OUT OF THIS WORLD
PAPER AIRPLANES

TAKUO TODA and ANDREW DEWAR

TUTTLE Publishing
Tokyo | Rutland, Vermont | Singapore

Contents

The Sky Is the Limit! **4**
My Friend Takuo Toda **5**
Can You Top This? **6**
Going for the Record **7**
    Competition Rules
How I Got Started **8**
    How I Design Planes
Paper Airplane Design Tips **12**
    A Paper Airplane Museum
    Ready for Takeoff!
Paper Airplanes in Orbit **16**
    Flights at the Edge of Space
    Teaching JAL to Fly
    Flying Around the World
Basic Paper Airplane Folding Techniques **24**
    Test Flying Your Planes
    Going Up!
    Diving for Speed
Fun and Games with Your Planes **30**
    Safety First!
    The Ring Toss Game
    The Curling Game
    Organizing a Contest
    Types of Competitions
    Open Contests
    Single Design Contests

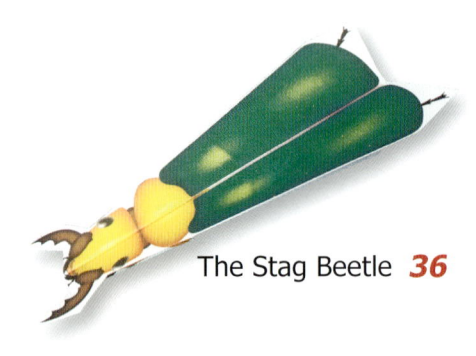

The Stag Beetle **36**

The Flyer **38**

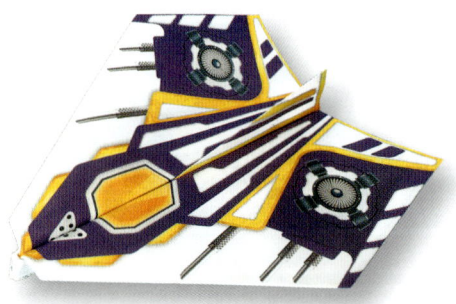

The Shooter **40**

The Relay **34**

The Cadillac **42**

Icarus **44**

The Flying Crane **46**

The Zero Fighter **48**

The Trident **50**

The Wave Rider **53**

The Ray Brick **56**

Jupiter Space Shuttle **60**

The Sky Is the Limit!

I have been folding and flying paper airplanes seriously for over forty years. Along the way, I discovered that there are many things you can do with origami, but paper planes are different from ornaments or representational models. The paper material is the same, and it's just your fingers folding the paper into various shapes, but once you launch the origami airplane into the air, you realize how much more there is to it than just folded paper. The sky is literally the limit!

I started out folding origami airplanes from diagrams in a book, but I soon began to feel I wanted to go beyond ready-made designs and started creating my own originals. Then, when that started getting easier, I began to fold a three-dimensional space shuttle, which no one had ever done before. It took a while, but the space shuttle paper airplanes are now my trademark.

The space shuttles looked like they belonged in space. So I went to the Japanese Aerospace Exploration Agency (JAXA) and they passed my designs on to NASA, who agreed to fly them back to earth from orbit.

My planes began to fly better than most other published designs. How much better? I took them to a stadium and broke the world record for time aloft. Twice!

My adventure all started with reading a paper airplane book. Now you have *this* book in your hands and it's your turn. Fold them all! Then create your own!

Did I say the sky is the limit? That's not quite right. Because it turns out that for paper airplanes, there is no limit at all!

—*Takuo Toda*

Above: One of my paper airplanes mounted on a boom suspended below a weather balloon at the edge of space. See page 20 for the full story.

Right: Posing alongside a huge example of my trademark design.

My Friend Takuo Toda

I have known Takuo Toda for about twenty years, since shortly after he published his first book in Japan. We have collaborated on several books since then. I started out with cut-and-paste paper gliders, a completely different type of paper airplane, but over the years I have absorbed a lot of origami knowledge from him, which has made it possible for me create my own origami airplanes.

Takuo's designs are quintessentially Japanese. What exactly makes Japanese origami airplanes different? This is something I often get asked. Certainly origami planes and paper gliders are much more popular in Japan than perhaps anywhere else. I would say that Japanese origami airplanes tend to be softer-looking, gentler, and more suited to flying in small spaces than Western darts. They often have that distinctive belly button on the bottom (see The Zero Fighter, page 48). The space shuttle designs with 3-D fuselages are unique to Japan. There are lots of whimsical planes, and there are planes that can fly for amazing lengths of time. Takuo's designs are completely representative of Japanese origami airplanes, but that's not an accident—he is the most imitated designer in Japan!

I have always thought it unfortunate that, despite Takuo's world records, and despite the fame he won for his hypersonic wind tunnel experiment, his designs are almost completely unknown outside Japan. They are imaginative, daring, polished, and amazingly high-performance, and they have had a huge influence in Japan. Now it's time they took flight all around the world!

We have collected some of his best planes for this kit. The current world record holder and three of Takuo's trademark space shuttle designs are here. But so are many very simple planes, and a few whimsical ones.

It is my pleasure to introduce Takuo and the many amazing things he has done.

Andrew Dewar

Can You Top This?

BY TAKUO TODA

I have held the Guinness World Record for time aloft since 2009. It was a long time coming, and I am very proud of it, but I would love to have it soundly broken by some younger person. It is close to 30 seconds, but no one seems to be able to break that barrier.

The Guinness time aloft record was first set in 1975 by William Pryor with a time of 15.0 seconds, and since then it has been broken by several people—Ken Blackburn (four times), Chris Edge, Andy Currey, and me (twice). My latest time is almost twice the first record, and it is getting close to the practical limit.

There are several challenges that need to be overcome if you want to break a record. You must have a good paper airplane. It has to glide very well, but also climb vertically towards the ceiling when thrown hard—most planes just loop. Then, you need a very large indoor space. School gymnasiums are far too small—the planes crash into the walls and ceiling. You need ideal weather; cold and dry. Hot air is less dense and gives less lift, and damp air warps the plane. And perhaps most of all, you need a good throwing form.

All of these finally came together for me on April 11, 2009, at the Big Rose event hall in Fukuyama, Japan—a cavernous room with a high ceiling and fairly still air. I was flying my Sky King design, and I had been doing strength training and throwing practice. Under the gaze of the judges and timers, I made ten throws. On one, the plane rose to within inches of the ceiling and began circling slowly down, just missing the wall at each pass. When it finally touched the floor, the timers let out a cheer. The flight was 27.9 seconds, 0.3 seconds longer than Ken Blackburn's eleven-year-old record.

But I wasn't completely happy, because 0.3 seconds isn't very decisive. I was sure I could fly longer than that. The chance came on December 19, 2010, at an event in the Sapporo Dome. The immense covered stadium could hold several Big Rose event halls, but it can also be humid and drafty. I had a new plane, The Zero Fighter (included in this kit, page 48), which has even bigger wings and lower drag than the Sky King. I aimed for the roof, the plane shot up and soared over the field, and when it finally landed, the time was 29.2 seconds. I had beaten my own record!

Winding up to launch a paper airplane for my attempt to break the longest flight duration record.

Going for the Record

BY ANDREW DEWAR

Once you have folded some of the high performance paper airplanes in this kit, and you know how to trim and fly them, it's time to think about going after a record.

But you can't just wind up, throw your plane, and claim to be best in the world. There are rules about what kind of planes are acceptable, about how and where the flights can be made, and about how the record is to be measured and judged. These rules are necessary to make it fair for everyone. They are summarized here, along with some of the reasons behind them, but you should look up the full text and read it carefully before making a formal attempt.

Julian Chee Yie Jian demonstrating his paper airplane throwing technique at a Red Bull contest. Photo courtesy Red Bull / Kumail Rizvi and Julian Chee.

Competition Rules

Duration flights must be made indoors, to prevent a lucky thermal updraft or gust of wind from giving the plane a helping hand.

You will need two independent judges to make sure the rules are enforced and to measure the flight time. You will also need someone to take a video showing the entire flight from launch to landing. Guinness won't recognize a record without the video.

You may make ten attempts, which includes fouls but not flights deemed unmeasurable by the judges. This is to prevent siege assaults on the record and reduce stress on the judges.

The plane must be made of one sheet of A4 or letter-size paper of less than 100 gsm weight. It can be cut, but the parts removed cannot be reattached. You can use cellulose tape totaling no more than 25 mm by 30 mm in size, cut or whole, to fasten folds, but for no other purpose. This rule prevents gaining an advantage by using specialized materials or designs. Everyone will be flying roughly similar origami airplanes.

The airplane is to be flown by one person, standing still on a level floor with both feet on the ground. The launch point must be level with or lower than the landing point. This rule is intended to equalize flying conditions and neutralize handicaps.

The flight time is measured from the moment the airplane leaves the thrower's hand until it first touches the floor or any other object. If any object helps the airplane in flight, the judges will call a foul. The time is measured with digital stopwatches to a hundredth of a second, and the two times are averaged and rounded to a tenth of a second. If the judges can't agree on a time, as when it isn't clear to both whether the airplane struck an object, for example, the flight is considered void.

If any of the ten attempts exceeds the current record, the thrower must send signed statements from the judges, the video, and color photographs (and newspaper clippings, if possible), to Guinness for independent corroboration and authentication.

How I Got Started

BY TAKUO TODA

Even the most consuming life-long skill or hobby has to start somewhere. But often it starts off as no more than a casual interest.

Many serious enthusiasts first encounter their speciality as children, but then set it aside when they get busy with school and friends. It's only when they rediscover it as an adult that their passion really takes off. So it was with me. A story in a Kindergarten magazine, about a mouse hiding in a carp streamer who has to learn to fly when it breaks loose, awoke my interest in origami airplanes. I folded many and flew them with my friends in high school. But an encounter in college turned paper airplanes into the focus of my life.

After high school I entered Gakushuin University to study mathematics, but it didn't suit me, so I transferred to a chemistry major at Waseda University. There, I took up mountain climbing with my friends. But in the fall of my first year I suddenly found myself weak and numb in my arms and legs, unable to walk straight or do much more than lie in bed. I later learned that the trouble was due to a pinched nerve in my neck, but at the time the cause was a mystery. I was told I had to stay at home and rest.

That left me with a lot of time to myself. Too much time! But by good luck I found an origami airplane book by Eiji Nakamura in a local bookstore. In no time I had folded all the planes in the book, and the pleasure I'd had as a child flooded back. But, none of the planes flew!

It was a shock. I couldn't understand why he would include the planes if they didn't fly. What was I missing?

At the back of the book I found Nakamura's address (the world was a little safer then), and discovered that he lived only 30 minutes from my dormitory. So, on a day I didn't feel quite so ill, I took the planes I'd folded and knocked on his door.

He wasn't expecting a visitor, and he certainly wasn't expecting a reader to complain that the airplanes didn't fly. But he must have thought that anyone who took the trouble to actually come to his house must be fairly serious. So he explained that his paper airplanes needed to be adjusted before they would fly well.

Nakamura's book had said nothing about adjusting the planes, but he spent the next few hours showing me how to do it. It was a revelation that paper airplanes are not just about folding. There is a lot of technique and skill involved, too.

Nakamura suggested I study aerodynamics, and he challenged me to try designing my own airplanes. He handed me a stack of origami paper—over one thousand sheets of paper! I could feel the weight of his expectations in that pile.

It was books like these by Eiji Nakamura that got me through my illness.

I imagine he would have been impressed if I'd folded up a dozen designs, and that's about all I thought I could manage. But I had nothing else to do, so I got to work.

I started with simple dart designs. Planes worth saving went into a cardboard box, and duds went into the garbage. After the darts, I began getting ideas for more interesting shapes, and the planes in the box piled up. When it was full—there were probably about two hundred planes in there—I went back to Nakamura's house.

During the first visit he had been indulgent, but this time he must have been astonished. I believe he felt that he had found both his rival and his successor, at the same time, and in the same person.

For my part, I was hooked. I folded and folded and folded. That was probably the most intensely creative time of my life. For two years I folded like mad, an average of thirty planes a day.

And even now, more than forty years later, I still fold every day, and new planes still go into the box.

How I Design Planes

Many people seem to think there's a kind of magic to designing origami airplanes, but there's no magic involved. In fact, it's mostly just fiddling with paper, folding and flying, folding and flying, and tossing the planes into either the box of successes or the recycling bin. But how exactly do you go about designing a new plane? For me, it is much more than just trial and error.

There are lots of types of paper airplanes, but over the years I have always specialized in origami. And I believe origami airplanes should be just folded. No cutting, no adding weight, no gluing. Any origami airplane design that requires anything more than folding is unfinished. I respect designers who make paper gliders (Andrew Dewar and I coauthored a book that contained both types of airplanes), but folding-only is my policy.

Above: A tiny representative sample of the many origami sheets that have gone into prototyping my planes over the years.

Right: My attic workspace, circa 1999. Note the planes hanging from the ceiling!

A diagram drawn by Takuo for a children's magazine.

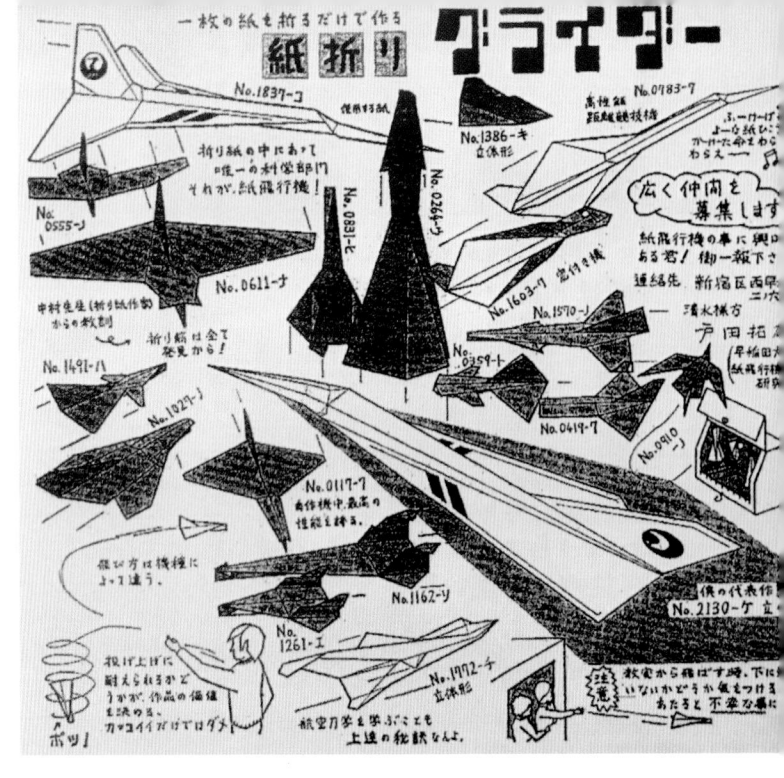

One of the reasons I prefer origami is that it can be done anywhere by anyone. As long as you have a piece of paper, you can make a plane—at home, at work, during a contest, even sick in bed.

When I'm designing a new plane, I make the first fold on impulse, and then just continue adding more folds from there. If I don't like them I change the angles or numbers of folds until I get a plane that flies. It's really as simple as that.

But quite often I find myself recreating something I've already designed, because familiar folds are creased right into my brain, and I follow the same path instinctively. If that happens, I start again with a different fold.

That said, I try to build up my repertoire of folding sequences: tricks for pinching in, bulging out, doubling up, making fins and tails, and so on. Then I can combine them, and new ideas pop up.

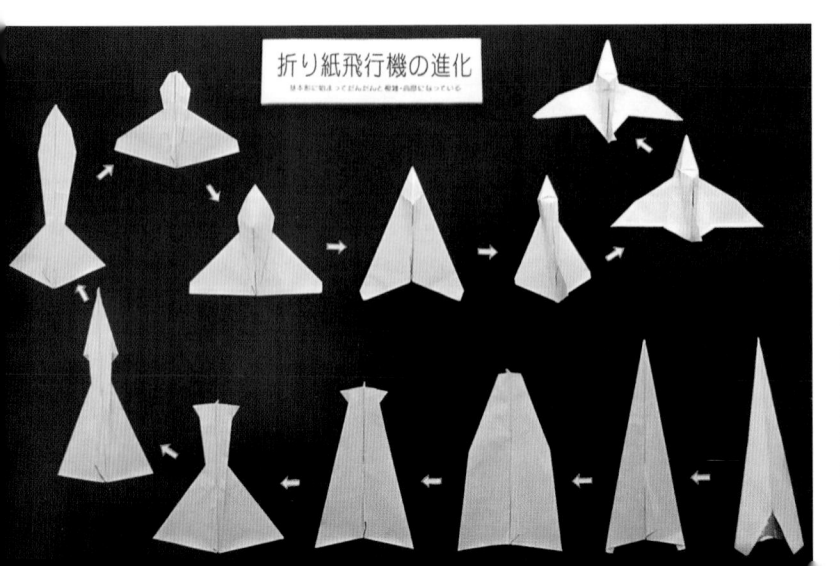

A display board in my museum showing the evolution of my planes from a simple dart through the shuttle to a realistic, three-dimensional space plane.

Unfortunately, they tend to pop up late at night, when I'm sleepy and just want to go to bed. It is then that the little worries of the day are gone and there is room for sudden inspiration. That's when many of my best planes are born.

I rarely have a specific goal in mind when I design. Many origami artists set out to fold a specific form, and they keep folding and adjusting until they get what they want. For paper airplanes, that's too much trouble, and it rarely works out well. I usually just wing it! It's not a very glamorous way of designing, but it works!

The exception to this is my space shuttle plane. It has become my trademark, and it is the design I'm most proud of. While I was still stuck in bed with my illness, it became clear that designing origami airplanes was what I really wanted to do; my life's work. But I needed to fold something unique and really amazing to justify what I was doing. At that time, NASA was just starting to fly space shuttles, and I thought, "I bet I can fold one." But I wanted it to be three-dimensional, like the real vehicle. I started to fold with that goal in my mind.

No matter how much I thought about it, though, I couldn't see how to do it. Then one day I noticed a little horizontal crease. Could it be pushed down to make a cockpit? I started folding, just following my intuition as always. And it didn't let me down. It took only an hour of folding to complete that first space shuttle.

I have built upon that basic design since then, and created lots of different versions of the shuttle (there are three in this kit, in fact), but it was born in those few frenzied minutes of folding. It is a rare case of an occasion when I actually "designed" a plane, though. Most of my airplanes are not so much designed, as discovered.

Above left: An early version of my space shuttle design.

Above right: My trademark plane, the space shuttle, took only an hour to design!

Right: An ever-growing pile of paper airplane designs.

Paper Airplane Design Tips

BY ANDREW DEWAR

Trial and error are good enough to get started. After all, the very first paper airplanes were created that way. It's unlikely that the classic "schoolboy dart" was "designed," for example, because there are pictures of it from long, long before the Wright Brothers' first flight. But as you get used to folding and flying, you will start to notice what works and what doesn't. Here are a few tips to get you started in the right direction.

Every new airplane begins with a single fold—usually the center fold. If using square paper, your first fold can either be straight from side to side, or diagonal from corner to corner. A diagonal center-line gives you a longer plane with a pointy nose, short, triangular wings and maybe a swept-back tail. Folding straight across the paper creates a shorter, blunter plane.

Rectangular paper can be folded in either direction, to give you a long, narrow plane that flies fast, or a plane with wide wings that flies slowly and gracefully.

Other center folds are possible (like the Trident fold), but get comfortable with the basics before trying them. Or, just go for it!

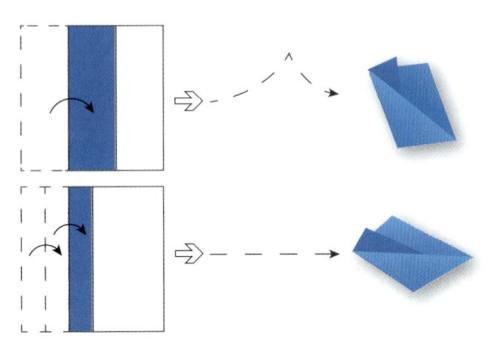

Your first concern will be balance. The nose should be heavyish, to put the center of gravity in the right place. If the nose is too light, the plane will flip up and stall. (If the nose is a tiny bit too heavy, you can adjust the back of the wing and get away with it.) Make the nose heavier by adding more folds at the front, and by keeping as much paper as far forward as possible.

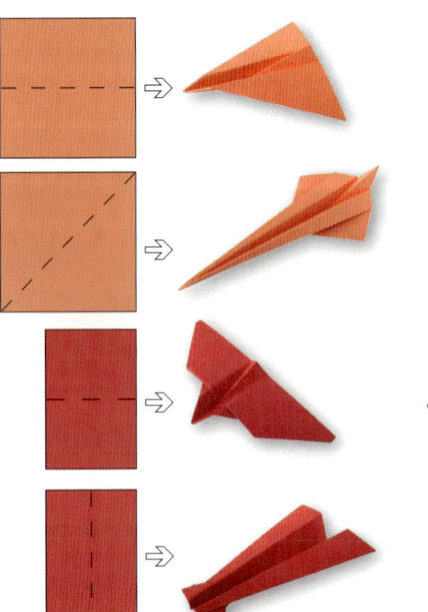

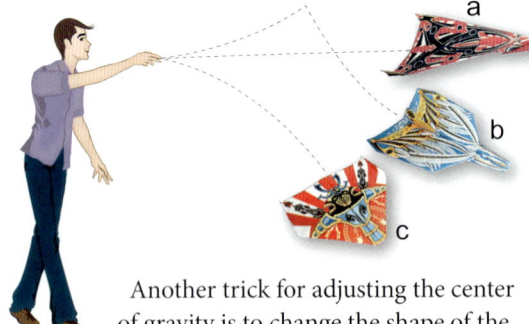

Another trick for adjusting the center of gravity is to change the shape of the wings. If the plane stalls, as in pattern b, make the wings smaller at the front. This moves the center of lift back. If the plane dives like pattern c, make the wings bigger at the front or smaller at the back. If the plane flies like pattern a, don't touch a thing!

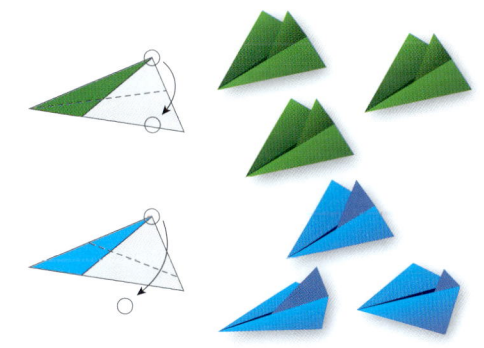

Using landmarks

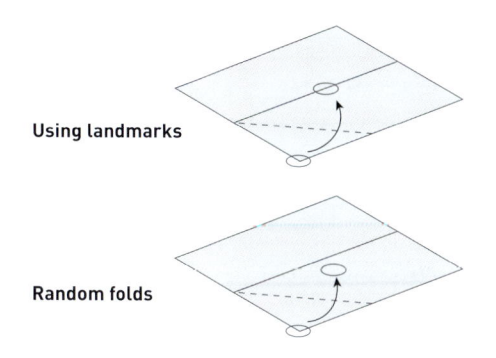

Random folds

You'll probably notice, when you start folding the planes in this kit, that every design uses "landmarks" to help you know where to fold. Why? Reproducibility. If your design is any good, you'll want to make more of it. And if you want to try for a time aloft or distance record, you'll probably need to fold and fly dozens or hundreds of them. If you design your plane with corners touching corners, edges meeting edges, sides folded in half, and other landmarks that show exactly where to fold, you can make as many copies of it as you like, and so can someone else! If you ignore the landmarks and just fold at random, you might make an amazing plane, but it will be unique; you won't be able to make another quite like it.

You also need to be sure you have enough rudder or a big enough fin at the back of the fuselage to keep the plane going straight. If the fin area is too small, the plane will spin and crash. If it flies for a little bit and then veers to one side no matter what you do, it's still too small. You can make it bigger by making the wings a little smaller. Or add wingtip fins.

Fold and fly, fold and fly, fold and fly. Make little changes each time and see how they affect the flight.

Not all of the planes will work out. Don't worry! It's just paper! If you wad them up and shoot some baskets, they'll still be lots of fun.

A Paper Airplane Museum

When you start designing your own paper airplanes, you will discover a big problem. You'll have a lot of great designs that you need to keep, and not enough shelves to hold them.

For Takuo, the solution was to build a museum! And so, in 2001, that's what he did. He had a small two-story building constructed close to his home and business in Fukuyama. Besides display space for thousands of airplanes, it has a small space for classes, and a shop selling books and paper. It started as a center for his paper airplane activities, but now is visited by school children, families, and paper airplane enthusiasts from around the world.

Ready for Takeoff!

When the Japanese government was offering seed money for projects to stimulate rural areas, the village of Toyomatsu, deep in the mountains above Fukuyama, proposed a paper airplane tower. The idea caught the imagination of government officials, and the village was able to build an 85 foot (26 m) tower on the top of Mt. Yonami (2,175 feet / 663 m). It was opened on March 21, 2003—the day after the very first National Origami Airplane Contest in Fukuyama.

The base of the tower contains a workspace where visitors can fold their airplanes. 59 feet (18 m) above that is an observation floor with windows opening out onto the mountainside in four directions. Planes flown through the windows

Top left: The Paper Airplane Museum in Fukuyama.

Top right: There's even room in the museum to show off planes by other designers.

Left: The museum has become the center of Takuo's activities. Here he is being filmed for a Japanese TV program.

soar out over the forest, circling and getting smaller and smaller until they disappear from sight. Because so many planes get lost in the forest, the tower provides a special paper that biodegrades quickly. When you start flying paper airplanes outdoors, you become very aware of the sky, trees, and rivers, and how important it is to keep them clean. And there is nothing like watching a pair of white wings soaring over a distant forest!

Top: Visitors can fold planes on site. Solar panels and wind generators provide all of the power, and the toilets are environmentally friendly, too.

Above: The forest extends out to the horizon in all directions, right to the distant mountains. Imagine your plane floating in this sky!

Left: The Toyomatsu Paper Plane Tower is the only facility of its kind in the world.

Paper Airplanes in Orbit

BY ANDREW DEWAR

Paper airplanes have been flown in space several times. Japanese astronaut Mamoru Mohri flew one on the space shuttle in 1992. Koichi Wakata, another Japanese astronaut, flew two on the International Space Station in 2009, one of which was a space shuttle paper airplane of Takuo's own design. And Brian Binnie tossed one around the cabin of the SpaceShipOne during one of its flights into space in 2004. But all of them were flown "indoors," where there was air but little gravity, so they didn't really fly at all. Without gravity, there is nothing to balance the wings' lift, so the airplane floats up to the ceiling and stops. What would happen out in space? Could it return to Earth and land safely like a real space shuttle?

Above: Koichi Wakata flew paper airplanes aboard the International Space Station in 2009. Photo credit JAXA/NASA.

Below: Can orbiting paper airplanes slow down enough to survive reentry without burning up?

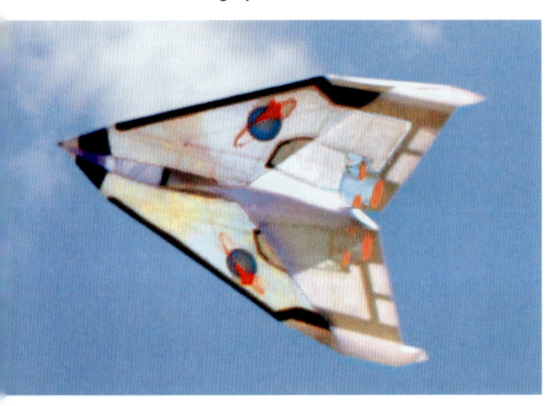

The plane would be fine as long as it stays in orbit, though it could not be said to be flying. It would be traveling at Mach 25, which is 25 times the speed of sound, or about 30 times faster than a jumbo jet. The very thin air at the International Space Station's altitude would slow it down enough that it would drop down into the thicker atmosphere below, where air friction would start to heat it up.

Extreme heat is the enemy of all things that fall from space. It's the reason that meteors glow and burn up as they fall. It's the reason the Apollo capsules had thick heat shields, and why the space shuttles were covered with insulating tiles. So a paper plane entering the atmosphere at orbital speeds would burn up instantly. Right?

Takuo didn't think so.

When the space shuttle Columbia broke up and crashed in 2003, the dangers of reentry were made very clear. But along with the scorched and melted items recovered from the crash were many manuals and sheets of paper that were found intact and unburnt. They were somehow saved from incineration despite their speed at the time. It seems that the paper items were light enough that they decelerated almost instantly to a speed slow enough that they didn't heat up.

So, in theory, a paper airplane hitting the thin upper atmosphere would slow down so much, so fast, that it could fly home safely.

That was Takuo's theory. He was sure it would work, but he wanted proof.

Takuo writes, "I first saw the space shuttle on TV half a year after the first flight, and my first thought was that NASA had designed it to look just like my paper airplane! It seemed like too much of a coincidence. I thought, what if my plane could fly in space too?

"In the course of my paper airplane activities I had come to know Professor Shinji Suzuki from the Department of Aeronautics and Astronautics at Tokyo University. One day I mentioned my dream to him. The logistical problems were obvious—how were we going to get the planes into space, and how would they be launched, for example—but to my surprise, Prof. Suzuki didn't think the paper airplanes would burn up. In fact, he thought my design was just about ideal.

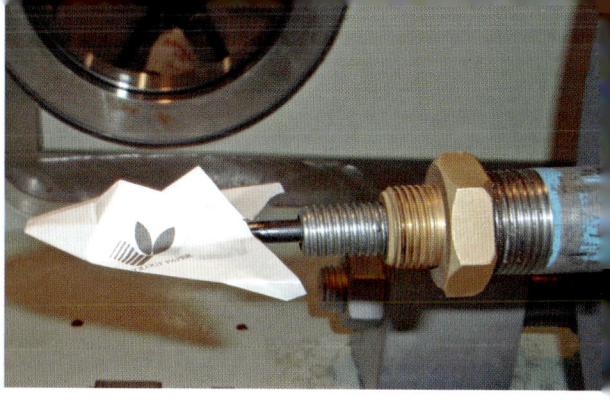

"So he agreed to do a test. Tokyo University has a hypersonic wind tunnel which was perfect for our experiment. It can create a flow of air that simulates flight at Mach 7, more than enough to cause aerodynamic heating. The wind tunnel uses very small models—models just the size of a paper airplane, in fact!

"I wanted to fold the space planes using the same *bagasse* paper I always use, because it is made from sugar cane pulp, and returns to nature quickly if the plane gets lost. But we wanted to give it a little help. So we had a few sheets coated with a thin layer of ablative silicon, which would carry away some of the heat as the friction vaporized it. I folded a number of small space shuttle test models, and one was mounted in the wind tunnel.

Above: Takuo's test model inside the wind tunnel, ready to prove its ability to withstand reentry forces.

Left: Professor Suzuki, front row second from left. Takuo is sitting to his left.

Above: Monitoring the status of the model during the test.

Above right: The press gathered to document the test.

"On January 17, 2008, in front of a group of journalists, Professor Suzuki ran the experiment. For ten long seconds, a whoosh of hypersonic air blasted past the model. I held my breath as I watched. Would the paper burn? Would there even be anything left? But when the wind stopped, the plane was still there, almost unchanged!

"In my mind at least, the concept had been proven. The paper space shuttles would survive the reentry!"

The story was carried in newspapers and blogs around the world. Some mocked it as a stunt or pointless experiment, but most expressed amazement and intense interest. It seemed like such a bizarre thing to do, but it recalled for every person who had ever flown a paper airplane as a child, that wonderful dream of flying one from the highest place possible.

But there is a big difference between knowing something is doable, and actually doing it. In this case, Takuo would have to find a way to get his airplanes into space, and convince NASA to let an astronaut take them outside and throw them!

There were a whole fleet of obstacles.

First, there was the design of the plane itself. The planes couldn't be carried into space already folded, because they would take up too much room in the cargo rocket, so they had to be easily foldable by an astronaut in a small space. The planes couldn't be test flown in space, because they wouldn't fly straight in microgravity. The planes would have to be launched by hand from outside the space station, which meant there had to be a rack to hold the planes while spacewalking, and some way for the astronaut to grip and direct them with a bulky spacesuit glove on.

But all of those concerns where tiny compared to the big one: getting permission!

Takuo already knew the Japanese astronaut Koichi Wakata through paper airplane activities at JAXA, the Japanese space agency. When he learned that Wakata would be flying to the International Space Station in 2009, Takuo and Professor Suzuki proposed their idea to him. Wakata was willing to launch the planes, if JAXA and NASA agreed to put the activity on the flight manifest.

The presence of Professor Suzuki in the proposal gave it enough scientific credibility to count as a kind of experiment—not just a stunt. At the same time, the hypersonic wind tunnel fame gave the flights a pretty high public relations value, especially for JAXA, which was always trying to emphasise its Japanese-ness.

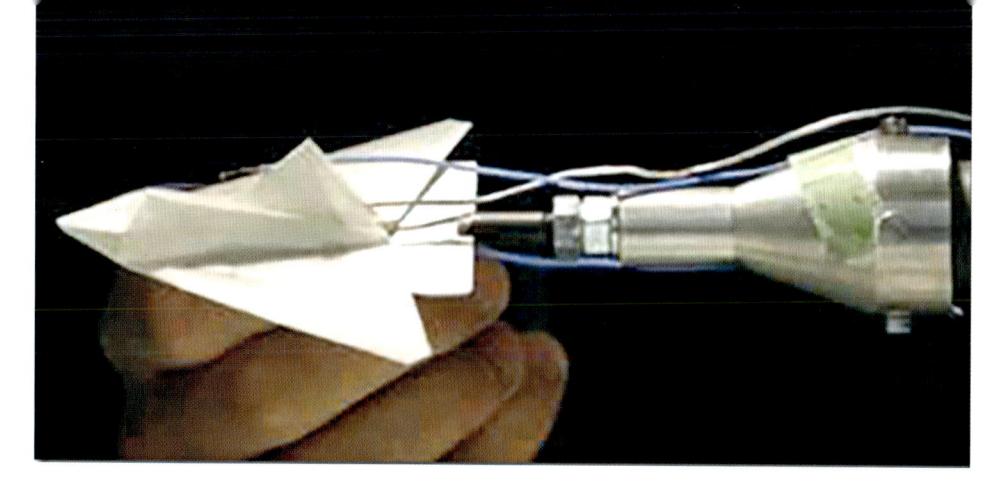

In March, 2008, JAXA granted permission. The proposal then went to NASA, this time with the backing of Japan. It would be a very high-profile, low-cost experiment that could be performed without too much special training or danger. NASA agreed.

Takuo and Professor Suzuki went into high gear. This was big news in Japan, so part of the preparation time went into creating a Japanese book of space shuttle designs.

Takuo took the basic Jupiter design (page 60) and made it suitable for space. It had to have a large tab on the bottom so it could be grasped with clumsy spacesuit gloves. It had to have the center of gravity moved backward slightly, so the nose would stay up on reentry and the plane would slow down quickly. It had to have a bigger rudder in order to stay stable at hypersonic speeds. And, of course, it needed Japanese flag insignia and messages for people who might find them.

In the end, NASA took the paper airplanes off the flight manifest, and Wakata only flew one origami space shuttle inside the station. The reason was that the planes would be untrackable, and NASA was forbidden by law from dropping things from orbit that would reach Earth but be uncontrollable. The planes would have remained in space for weeks or years before

Above: Mounting the test plane onto the wind tunnel harness.

Right: A signed photo and message from Koichi Wakata at the Fukushima Airport just days after the 2011 earthquake. The plane bears words of encouragement to those affected. Photo courtesy of Keiji Hamasaki.

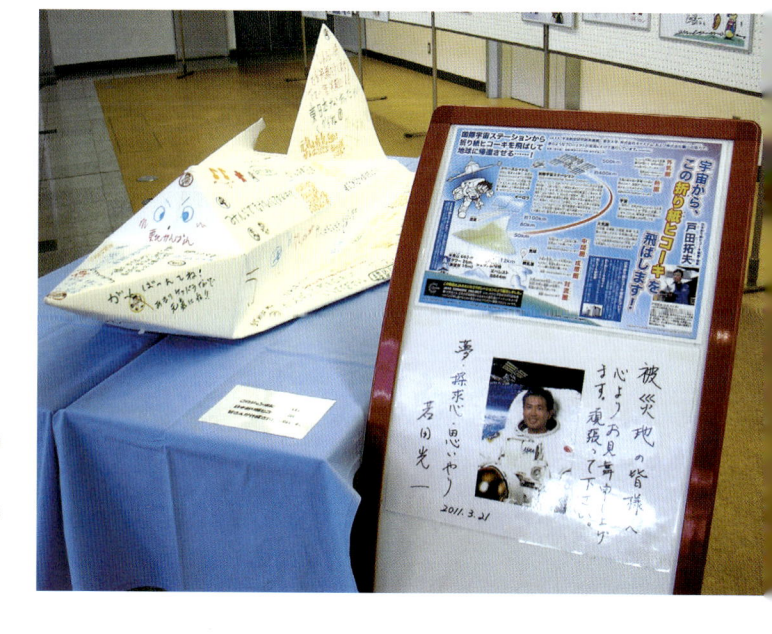

their orbits decayed enough to reenter the atmosphere, and then they might travel thousands of miles before landing. NASA and the U.S. government were worried that a landing in the wrong country might create an international incident.

Will the flights ever take place? Small tracking chips now available might make it possible to regain permission. Takuo certainly hasn't given up. So don't be surprised if, one day, you find a little origami airplane in your garden that looks a little charred and says it's just come back from space!

Flights at the Edge of Space

Japanese television loves quirky challenges, so it was only to be expected that Takuo's work on the space flight would lead to a request from a TV program to do the next best thing: fly paper planes back to earth from the edge of space.

"The edge of space" is a bit of an exaggeration, because no TV program could afford the rocket needed to boost planes the 62 miles (100 km) needed to reach it. Fuji Television wanted to use a weather balloon to carry paper airplanes as high as possible and release them for a program aired in 2014 called "Otona Asobi."

Takuo is a veteran of this type of program, and the theme, adults playing out childhood dreams, was right up his alley.

Naturally, he chose his Jupiter design (page 60). The balloon was expected to travel well into the stratosphere, and the planes would have to battle the 60 mph (100 km/h) winds of the jet steam. Jupiter's space shuttle configuration is ideal for that kind of speed and altitude.

Takuo folded ten planes in bright colors, and before they were put inside a small foam pod, they were covered with messages and requests to finders.

The pod was to protect the planes until they reached the peak altitude.

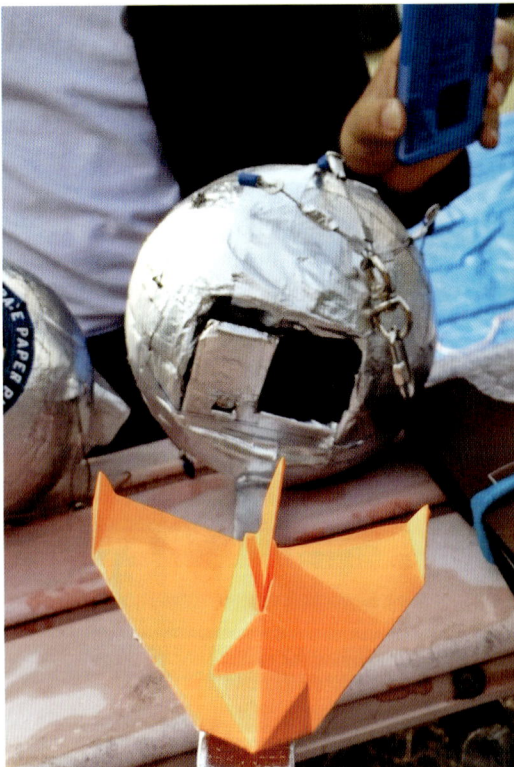

Top: The planes were placed into a foam pod for the trip to the stratosphere. They were covered with hopeful messages.

Above: The on-board camera looked out past a space shuttle plane at the end of a boom.

When the air got too thin, the balloon would burst, a door would open, the planes would spill out, and a camera would film them flying off.

As soon as the balloon was released, it sprang into the air with the camera and paper airplane pod hanging beneath it. In no time it was out of sight.

The camera pod carried a GPS transponder and a small parachute so it could be recovered. But to avoid any danger to people in case the parachute didn't open, most of the flight took place over the ocean.

The program staff thought there was only a 30 percent chance of recovering the camera—even with the GPS. They tracked it for 43 minutes until the signal suddenly went dead. The recovery team thought the camera was lost for good, but after five minutes of scanning the waves, one member shouted, "There it is!"

When the camera's video was played, the staff found it had captured the moment of release perfectly. The balloon and the pod were being buffeted by powerful winds, but the hatch opened and ten airplanes spilled out into the thin air and headed for Earth. The sky was deep indigo, almost black, and the horizon was curved (see photo, page 4). The balloon had climbed to almost 90,000 feet (almost 30,000 m); three times the height of commercial flights.

None of the airplanes were found, however. The wind was blowing them out to sea, and at the height they began their flight, they could have traveled hundreds, even thousands of miles.

The Guinness World Record for the highest flight is perhaps not as glamorous as those for time aloft and distance flown, but it is just as difficult, and requires large teams of people to achieve.

The rules for the highest flight do not require the plane to be launched by hand, so remote controlled devices attached to

The balloon and its cargo disappeared into the sky very quickly.

weather balloons are now the preferred technique. The planes are released so high that the balloon is invisible from the ground, and the planes can fly surprising distances before landing, so cameras and computers are needed to verify the launch. And because the balloons fly well above the level of commercial flights, special

Above: A crowd of new hires launching their careers.
Left: The crowd gathers to participate in a contest.
Below left: A flight attendant preparing for the contest.
Below: JAL staff brought their families for a day of fun.

permission is absolutely necessary.

The current record was set in 2015 by David Green and a group of students as a high school project. Their balloon burst 114,970 feet (35,043 m) above Elsworth in the UK, and scattered planes far and wide.

Teaching JAL to Fly

For many years now, Japan Airlines (JAL) has asked Takuo to help them train their staff, and he teaches the pilots, attendants, and ground staff how to fold and fly several kinds of paper airplanes. What does it have to do with running an airline? Well, if you can't fly a paper airplane, how do you expect to fly a jet?

Top right: Flying with a fan in Belgium.

Below: Turning a Chinese tower into a paper airplane tower.

Flying Around the World

Takuo's precision molding business takes him around the world, and wherever he goes, he takes his planes with him. He's found that a paper airplane, quickly folded and flown at a business meeting, makes a more lasting impression than any business card.

His own business has offices and factories in Thailand, the Philippines, Columbia, and even the United States. Not surprisingly, paper airplanes are becoming something of a fad in these countries. He runs workshops and sponsors contests, but sometimes the various governments become involved and help out. Paper airplanes are a safe and healthy pastime that everyone seems to love!

And he has been called to many other countries (France, Austria, and China in particular) to teach classes and pass on his enthusiasm.

Shown here are just a few examples of Takuo sharing his passion for paper planes around the world.

Basic Paper Airplane Folding Techniques

BY ANDREW DEWAR

These planes are all easy to fold, once you understand what the diagrams mean. The symbols are the standard ones used in all origami books.

Here's what the arrows mean:

Fold this way

Fold and reopen

Fold around behind

Flip the whole plane over

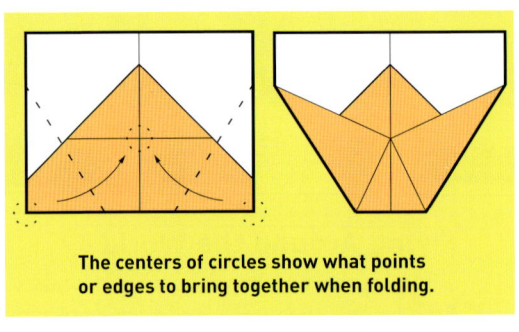

The centers of circles show what points or edges to bring together when folding.

There are only two ways to fold paper: mountain folds and valley folds. For valley folds, you fold the paper towards you. For mountain folds, you fold it away. But the origami paper in this book already has the folding lines printed on the front and back, so every fold is a valley fold! Just follow the numbers.

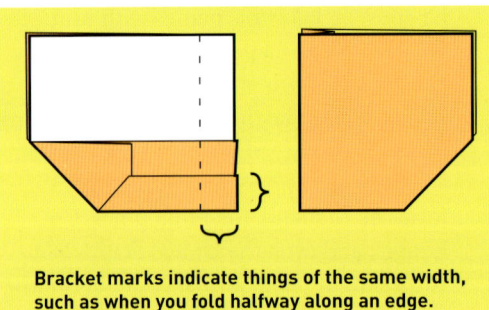

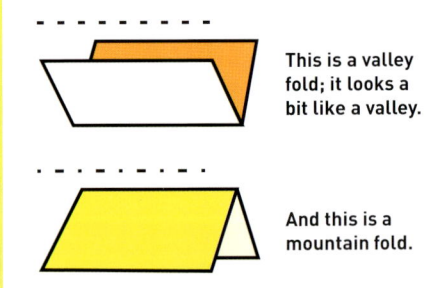

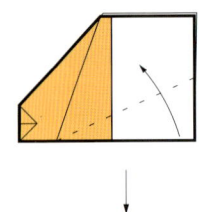

Bracket marks indicate things of the same width, such as when you fold halfway along an edge.

This is a valley fold; it looks a bit like a valley.

And this is a mountain fold.

Some of the planes have reverse-folded rudders. Here's how to make a reverse fold. First, fold and unfold the paper to crease it. Then open the plane out slightly and push the bit that will be the rudder inside. Recrease the folds, which have now been reversed from valley to mountain and from mountain to valley, and you're done. It's not hard at all!

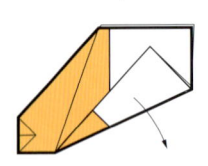

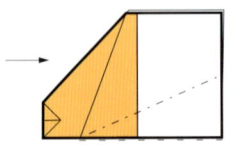

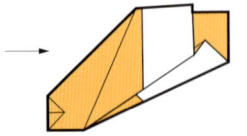

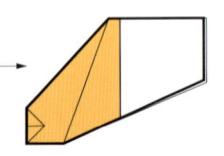

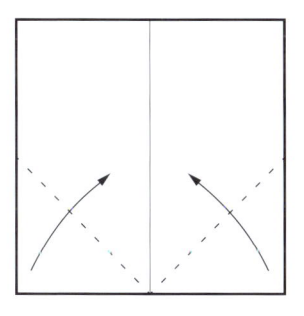

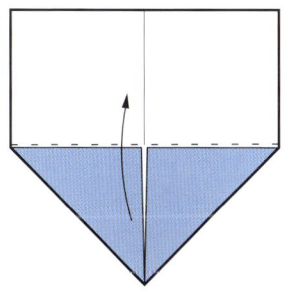

Most planes start with the paper face down. The drawings show the front of the paper in color, and the back in white.

Folding is a lot easier if you do it away from you. Line up the edges or corners carefully, double check, and then crease the paper. The best way is to start from the middle, and crease first to the left, then the right.

Finally, burnish the fold to make it really sharp. You can run your thumbnail along the crease, or use a tool, such as a pen cap.

Most of the planes need a final tweak to really fly well. They will dive until you bend up the back edge of the wing slightly. Bending the wing keeps the nose up and lets the plane float on the air. But too much, and it will stall and crash. Add and subtract until the plane flies just right.

Whenever possible, fold the paper away from yourself.

Your folds will be more accurate if you crease from the middle outward.

When you are sure the fold is okay, burnish it with your thumbnail to make the crease sharp.

The last step for each plane is to bend up the rear edge of the wings slightly for stability.

25

Test Flying Your Planes

Your plane won't fly very well unless it's straight. Hold it at arm's length and check. If it's out of alignment, carefully tweak the wings and tail until everything is straight and flat.

Test fly the plane by tossing it firmly straight forward and watching how it flies. If it stalls, dives, or turns, adjust it as shown on the facing page and test fly it again, until it glides gently.

Remember, these airplanes are made from paper, so they bend in crash landings, and warp in sticky weather. You will have to tweak them again from time to time. If they stop flying well, check that they are straight, test fly them again, and they'll go back to being great!

If your plane is out of alignment, make minor adjustments to change it from this...

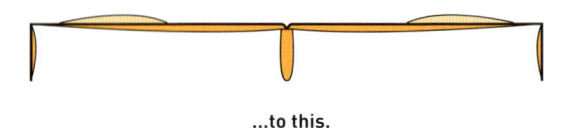

...to this.

Testing the Cadillac. Hold it just about where it balances.

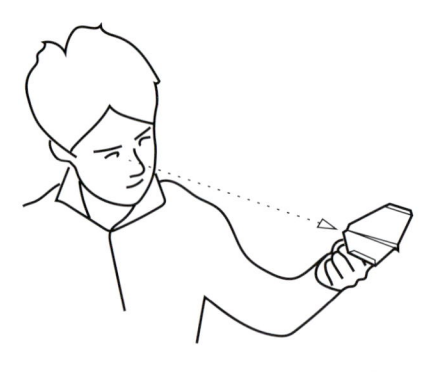

The plane should be straight, without twists

Throw your planes straight ahead, the way you would a dart.

Straighten the wings and tail

Some of the planes, like the Zero Fighter, can be thrown straight up. Don't forget the follow-through!

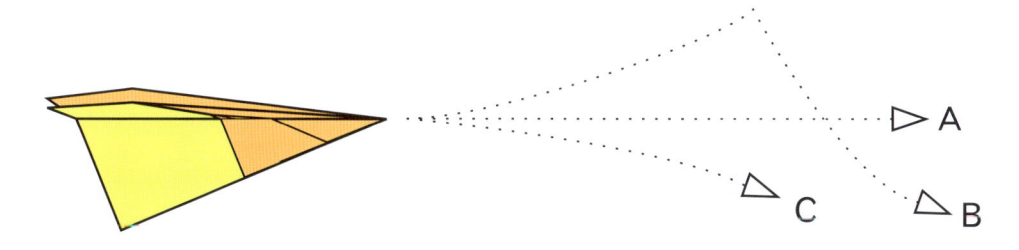

If your plane stalls or dives, adjust it until it glides straight, as in pattern A.

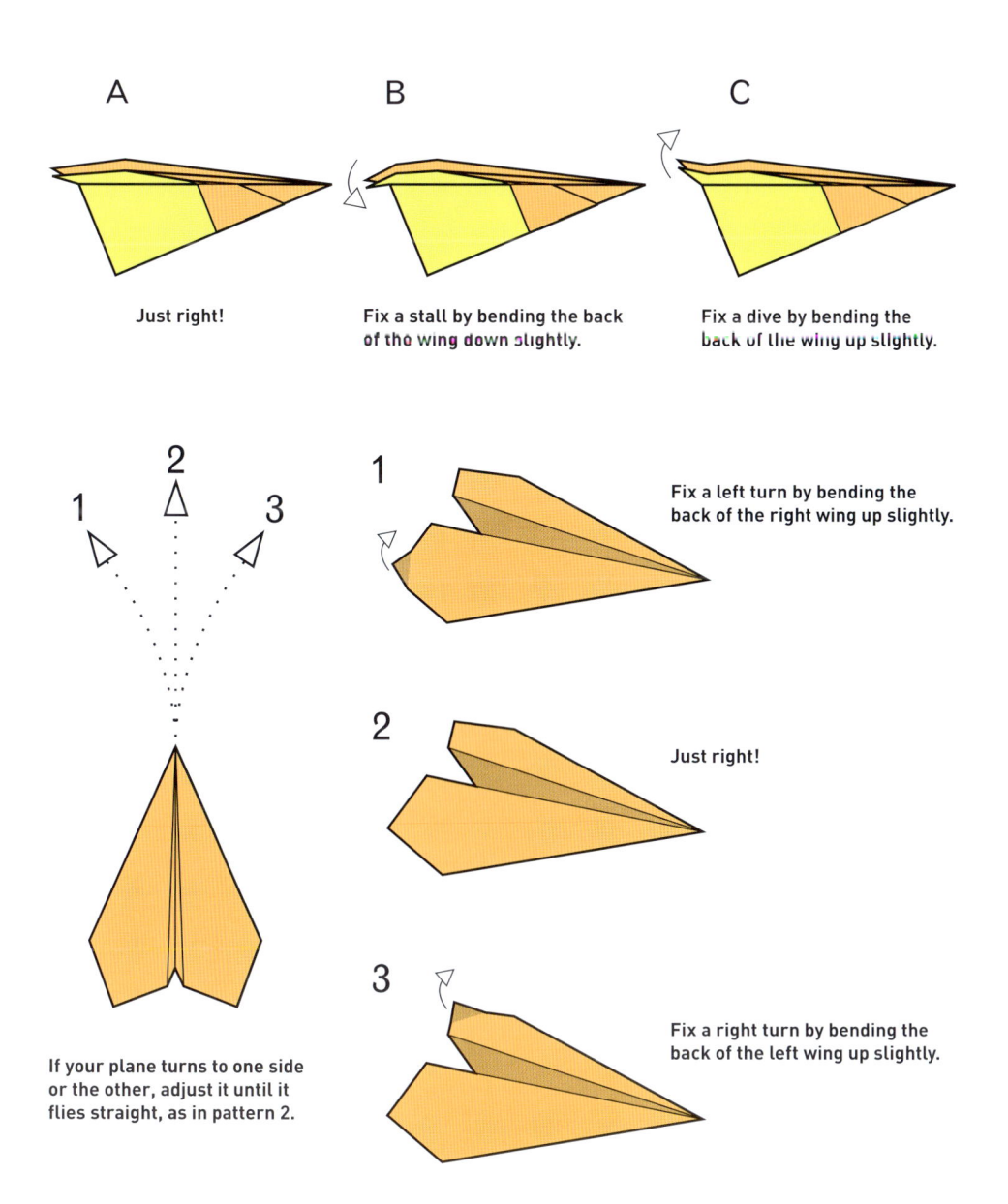

A

Just right!

B

Fix a stall by bending the back of the wing down slightly.

C

Fix a dive by bending the back of the wing up slightly.

If your plane turns to one side or the other, adjust it until it flies straight, as in pattern 2.

1

Fix a left turn by bending the back of the right wing up slightly.

2

Just right!

3

Fix a right turn by bending the back of the left wing up slightly.

27

Left: The Flying Crane (page 46) presents a uniquely graceful profile against a winter backdrop. What could be more Japanese than a wintering crane?

Below: Andrew Dewar demonstrates Takuo Toda's powerful and efficient throwing technique.

Going Up!

Champions and record holders throw with their whole bodies. They start crouched down with the plane all but touching the ground. Takuo pops up from the knees, so that the plane is slung up in a straight line quite close to his body. It is pointing upwards the whole time. Ken Blackburn, by comparison, twists his torso while springing up from the waist, and in some pictures it looks like he's bent right over backwards. His plane swings up in a long arc, quite far from his body core. Blackburn uses brute power, which his plane has to absorb; Takuo's smooth throw accelerates the plane cleanly.

When you throw high and hard, try to keep the plane heading straight in one direction through the whole launch. This will put less stress on the wings, and there will be very little warping or flutter. The plane will slice cleanly through the air as it rises. In fact, it will look almost like it's gliding vertically!

Kids are naturals; adults less so. Ironically, people who play lots of baseball and football sometimes have trouble throwing the planes without setting them rolling with a final snap. The secret is practice. Try holding the plane in different places. Try throwing at different angles. Try snap throws and smooth rolling throws. And when you find a style that makes the plane climb high or fly far, practice it!

Rest too. Too many throws in a row may tire or injure your arm, so don't overdo it. But don't under-do it, either!

Diving for Speed

If you throw a twisted cone of paper, it will go a long way. But not far enough. If you are throwing your plane for a record or in a competition, you want it to be more than just a wad of paper. The record set by John Collins and Joe Ayoob in 2012—226 feet, 10 inches, or almost 70 meters—was only possible because of the plane's special flight path.

If you want to throw a ball as far as possible, you need to throw it up at a 45 degree angle. That's the best angle for sending ballistic objects as far as possible. Throw at a bigger or smaller angle and it will fall short. That's because the ball follows an arc. It is slowing down and falling as soon as it leaves your hand. A plane like a dart with tiny wings will fly just the same way, up and down, no farther than you can throw it.

But a good distance-covering plane is thrown at a much smaller angle—almost horizontally—after which the lift from the wings makes it climb up almost to the ceiling. When the speed drops off, the plane noses down into a dive, and then, with the speed renewed by the dive, it flares into a long flat glide right across the room. In other words, the plane gets its flying speed from both your arm and the height to which it climbs. Getting the angle and throwing speed right to just miss the ceiling and lengthen the glide at the end is the secret to capturing records and winning contests.

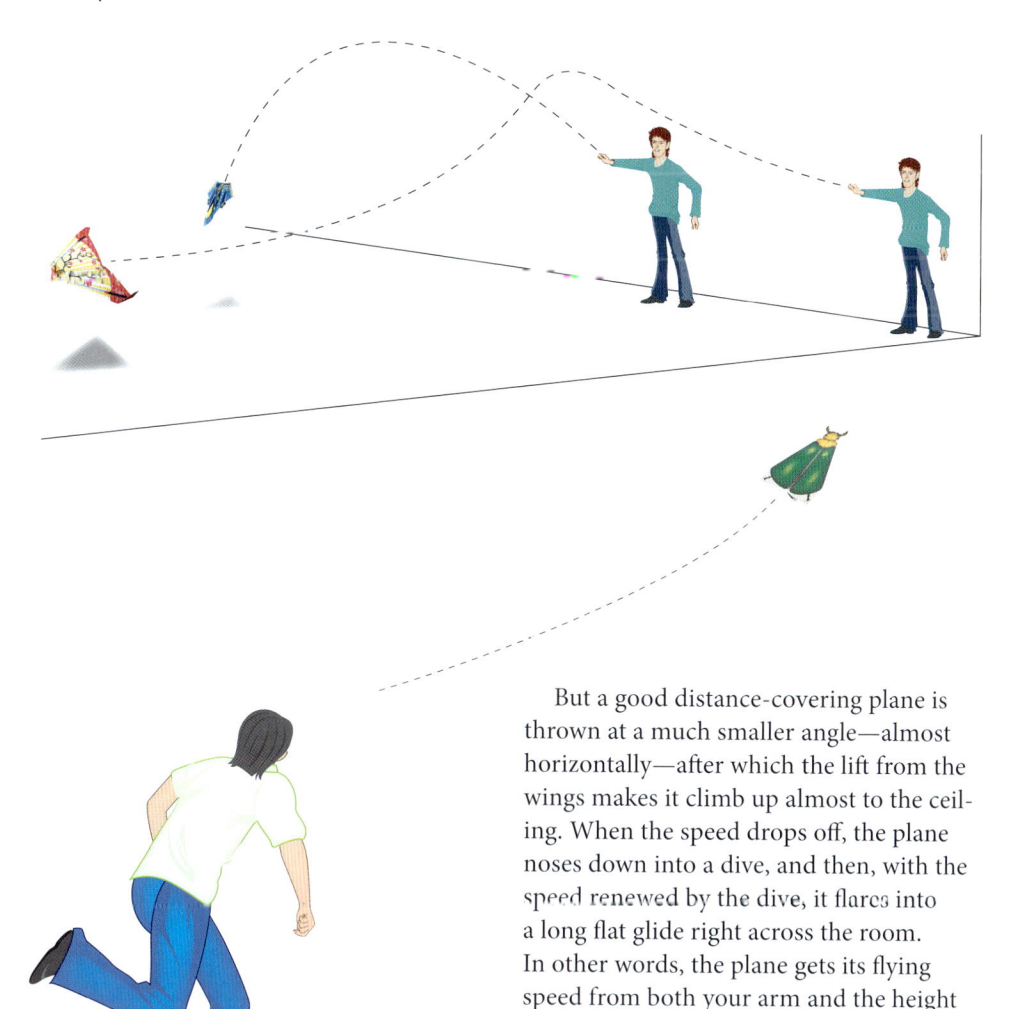

29

Fun and Games with Your Planes

BY ANDREW DEWAR

Once your planes are all folded up, you're going to be having fun flying them. But just tossing them around a room by yourself might start to get dull after a while. Why not get together with friends to play paper airplane games, or try competing to see who is the best paper airplane pilot? Here are some great games and contest hints.

Safety First!

Before we start throwing planes, let's think about safety. We can't say enough about it. Keep in mind that your planes are pointy and thrown at high speed, and you'll likely be flying them with other people around. Make sure you stay far enough away from others that your plane won't hit them. This is especially important in a contest, where everyone will be pushing the limits of the planes. Never throw your planes at people or animals. Stay away from busy streets and power lines, and don't go after planes that have landed in dangerous places. It isn't worth it! You can always just fold up another one!

The Wave Rider (page 53) riding a wave in the park.

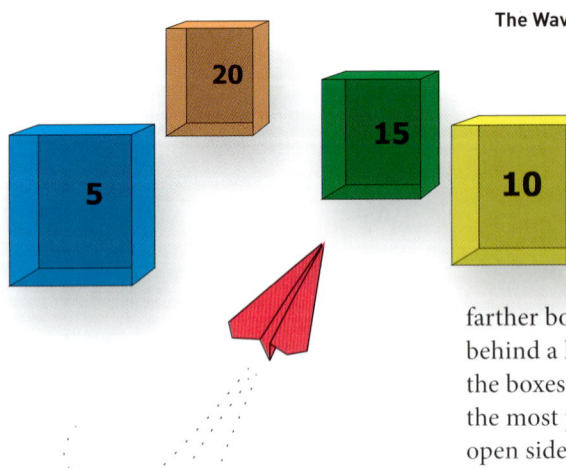

The Ring Toss Game

This game isn't exactly a ring toss, but it's the same sort of idea. Set up a number of open boxes of different sizes or at different distances. Smaller or farther boxes earn more points. Players stand behind a line and try to fly their planes into the boxes. Planes that go in get points, and the most points win. Turn the boxes so the open side is facing up if you want to make it even harder. Do you have some hula hoops? You could set those up too. You could also play using holes in a board, but planes tend to get bent if they crash into the board.

The Curling Game

To curl, you need a slippery wood floor, like a gym floor. Mark some bulls-eye circles on the floor with colored tape. Players form two teams, and take turns throwing their planes from behind a line (about 5 to 10 yards from the mark), trying to land in the middle of the bulls-eye. If there's a rival plane there already, knock it out of the way! You can either play for points, or let the plane closest to the center be the outright winner.

Left: Distinct against a snowy landscape, this is the Zero Fighter (page 48).

Below: World champion Takeshige Kishiura shows kids how to fold winners at the 2016 Red Bull Paper Wings World Finals.

The record-breaking Zero Fighter design (page 48) gliding on a spring breeze.

Organizing a Contest

Sooner or later, you're going to want to try competing with your friends to see who is the best paper airplane pilot. Here are some recommendations for contests, formal and pick-up.

Types of Competitions

Most paper airplane contests measure either the time or distance of flights.

Distance is judged by measuring in a straight line from the launch site to where the plane first touches the ground or a wall. The trick is in getting the plane to fly straight! Distance contests are fun in gymnasiums, but keeping track of flight distances outdoors is challenging, because wind and rising air can waft the planes a very long way!

If planes start going past the end of a fifty-yard tape measure, it is easier if you draw concentric lines at predetermined distances, and measure from the lines to the planes to extend your range. Contestants throw from one spot, with or without a run-up as you wish. How many times each contestant can throw, and whether you add the distances or just choose the best one, are rules you can set yourself.

Using a stopwatch to time flights is often easier. Start the watch the moment the plane is launched, and stop it when the plane touches the ground, hits an obstacle and stops, or disappears from sight. Judges might have to run a bit to keep the planes in view, but that's fun, too. You can choose the number of flights and scoring system you find easiest or best, as long as everyone competes by the same rules.

Open Contests

The most basic type of contest is the open contest, where any number of people can compete for the highest scores.

You can change the rules to suit the place and number of participants. For example, each pilot might make five flights, and the pilot with the highest total flight time wins. You can have a fly-off to break ties. A fun variant of this allows more flights, with only the best five scores added up. Why not try a mass launch, where everyone launches their plane at the same time, and the last one to land wins? If there are a lot of participants, you may need to line them up to fly in turn. But this can be boring, so I recommend a looser system of timing with lots of judges roving the site and timing when requested. This lets pilots fly when they are ready, at their own pace. You could even use an honor system and let pilots time each other. Record the scores on a time card, and add them up to find the winner.

Single Design Contests

Another type of contest is the Single Design contest, where everyone uses the same kind of plane and paper. This makes a great tie-in to a workshop or school activity; all the participants fold the same type of plane, and compete over trimming and flying skills.

Right: The Zero Fighter amidst the blossoms.

Left: Andrew Dewar throwing the Zero Fighter.

The Relay

BY TAKUO TODA

This plane is really easy to fold, but it can be tricky to fly. The reason is the expanse of one-layer-thick paper at the back, which tends to dip at the corners. Before flying it, inspect it from the front and carefully bend the wings so they are straight or bent slightly up. Sun and damp weather will make the paper misbehave, so if you can't seem to get it right, it's best to just wait for a better day.

1

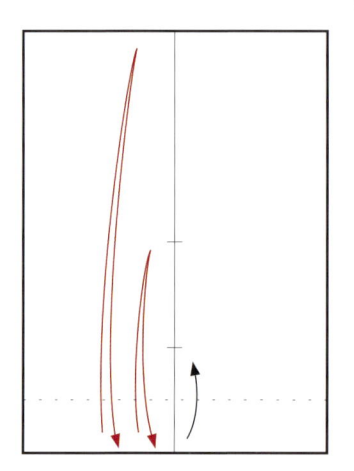

Start with the paper face down. Fold the bottom edge of the paper up on line 1. The red arrows show how to find the line if using plain paper.

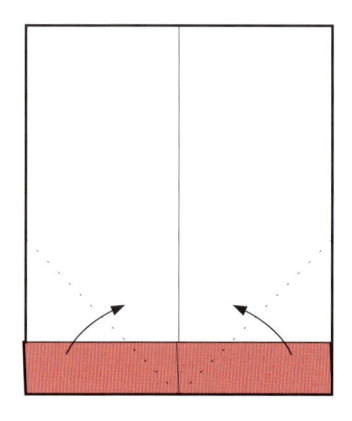

2

Fold the bottom corners in to the center line on the 2 lines.

3

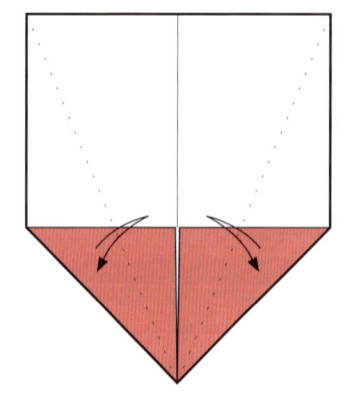

Fold the new corners in to the center line on the 3 lines, and unfold them.

4

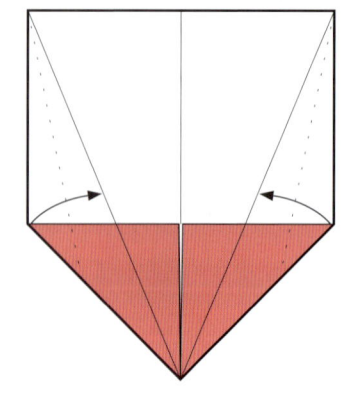

Fold the corners in to the creases you just made, on the 4 lines.

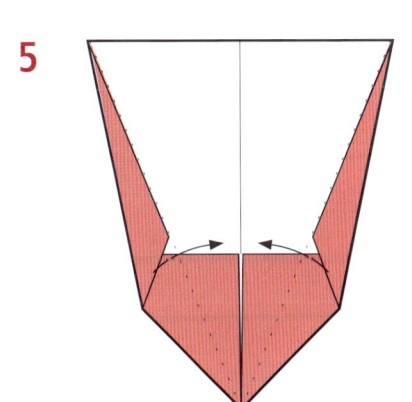

5 Refold on the 3 lines.

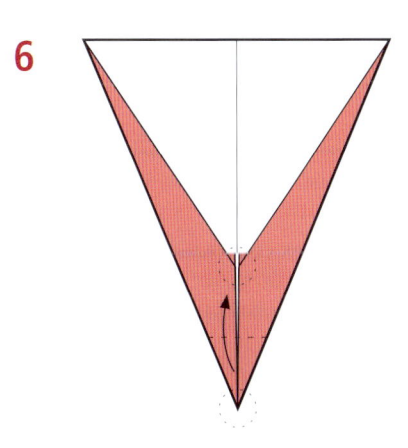

6 Fold the tip of the plane on line 5 to meet the corners indicated by the circle.

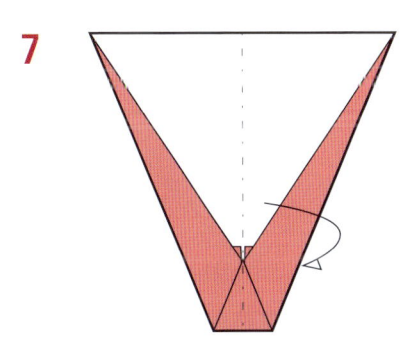

7 Fold the plane in half away from you.

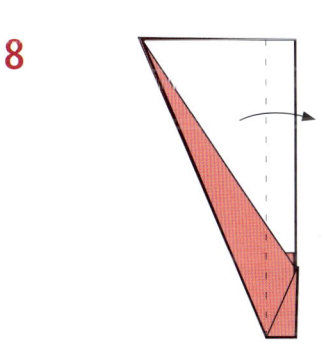

8 Fold the wings down on the 6 lines, starting at the bottom corner and parallel to the center line.

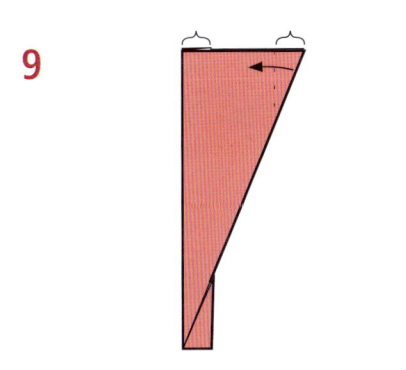

9 Fold up the wingtip rudders. The width of the rudders is the same as the fuselage.

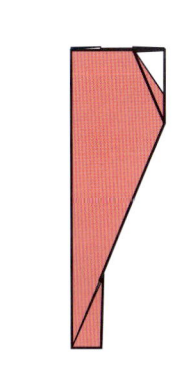

10 Straighten out the wings and rudders, bend up the rear edge of the wing a tiny bit, and you're done!

35

The Stag Beetle
BY TAKUO TODA

Japanese kids love to catch and raise beetles, and this plane looks like one of the most popular; the stag beetle. It starts as a "squid plane," but with a few more folds the front wings become the beetle's huge sideways-snapping jaws. It flies dead straight, and goes a long way with a good throw.

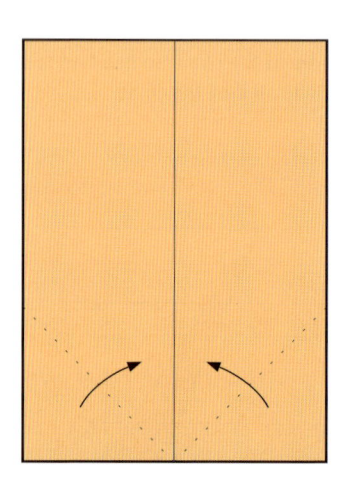

1

Start with the paper facing up, and fold the corners to the center line on the 1 lines.

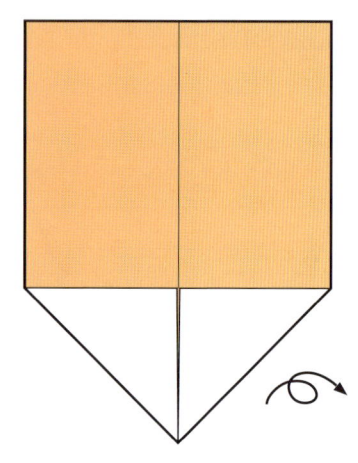

2

Flip the paper over.

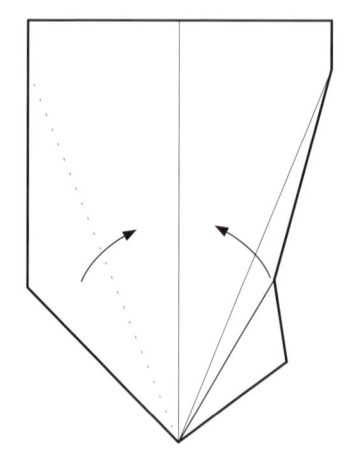

3

Fold the new corners to the center line on the 2 lines, but pull the first corners out from behind as you go. Step 4 shows how the results will look.

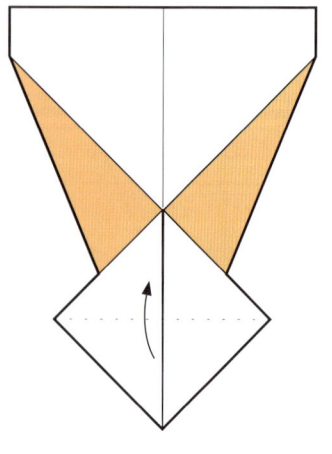

4

Fold the nose up on line 3.

36

5

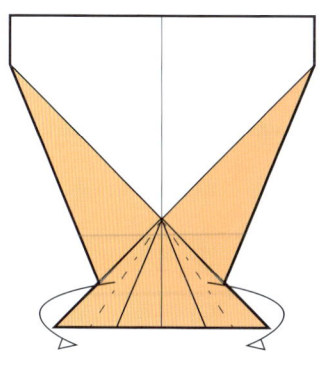

Mountain fold the free corners on the 4 lines. Step 6 shows how the results will look.

6

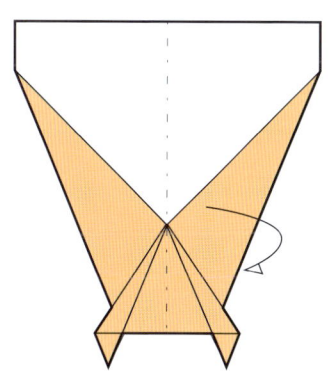

Fold the plane in half away from you.

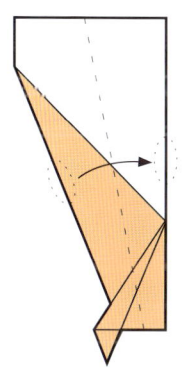

7

Fold the wings down on the 5 lines, so that the outer edges touch the center line.

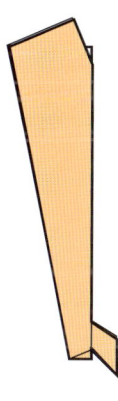

8

Straighten out the wings, turn up the back edge of the wing very slightly, and you're done!

The Flyer

BY TAKUO TODA

This plane is easy to fold and adjust, but once it's properly trimmed, it flies amazingly well. The center line crosses the short side of the paper, so the wings are long and relatively narrow. It has a kind of floating glide; long and beautiful.

1

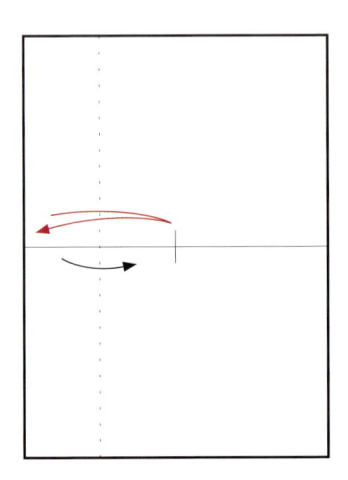

Start with the paper facing down. Fold the left edge to the center on line 1. The red arrow shows how to find the line, if using plain paper.

2

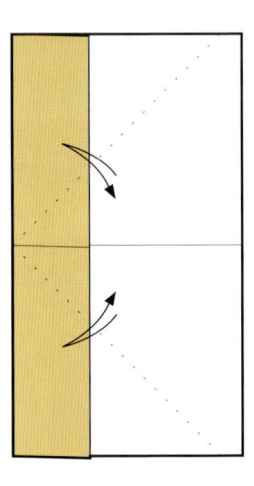

Fold the left corners to the center line on the 2 lines, and unfold them again.

3

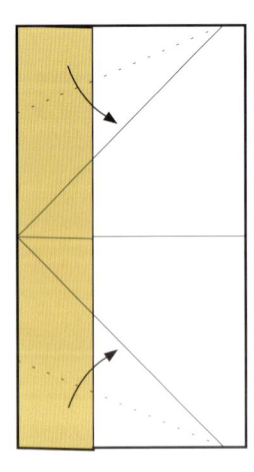

Fold the left corners on the 3 lines to the creases you just made.

4

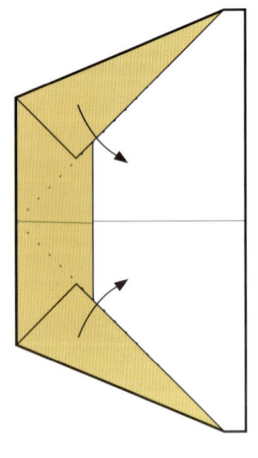

Refold the 2 lines.

38

5

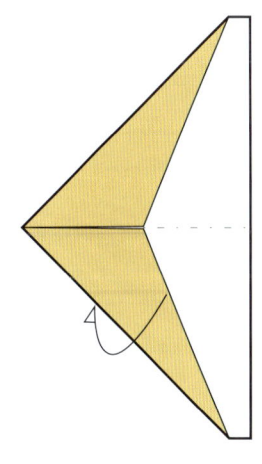

Fold the plane in half away from you.

6

Fold and unfold on lines 4 and 5. Line 4 starts where the paper gets thick.

7

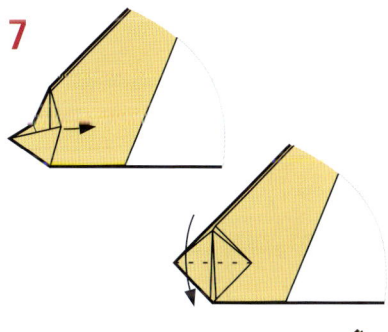

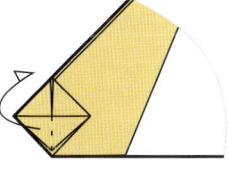

Put pressure on the nose of the plane to flex it open into a small scoop shape. Continue pressing to close the scoop, then pivot the resulting rhombus shape toward you so the model lies flat. Fold the tip down on line 6, and then fold the left half of the rhombus behind.

8

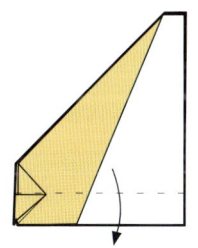

Fold the wings down on the 7 lines.

9

Fold the wingtip rudders up on the 8 lines. The width of the rudders is the same as the width of the fuselage.

10

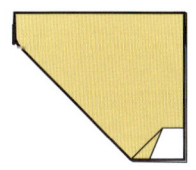

Straighten out the wings and rudders, bend up the back edge of the wing a very little bit, and you're done.

39

The Shooter

BY TAKUO TODA

The Shooter starts off like a belly-button plane, but then instead of folding the protruding triangle on the belly forward to hold everything together, there is a clever lock mechanism on the nose to do that. The result is a simple and robust plane that you can throw hard indoors and out.

1

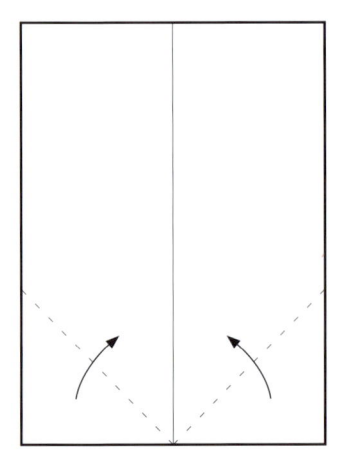

Start with the paper face down. Fold the bottom corners to the center line on the 1 lines.

2

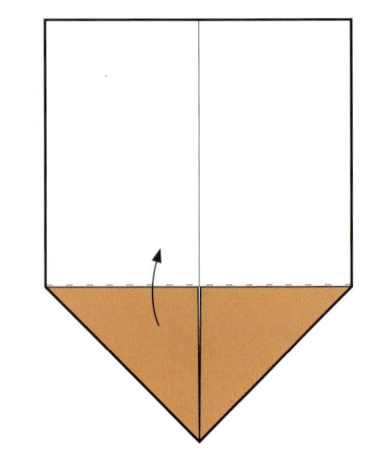

Fold the bottom of the paper up on line 2, starting at the new corners.

3

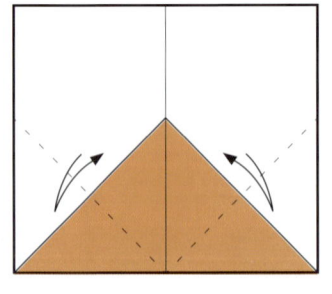

Fold the new corners to the center line on the 3 lines, and then unfold them again.

4

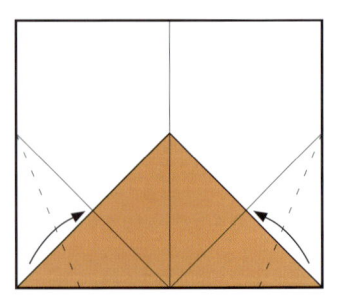

Fold the corners on the 4 lines to the creases you just made.

5 Refold the 3 lines.

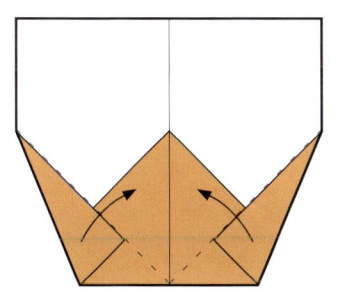

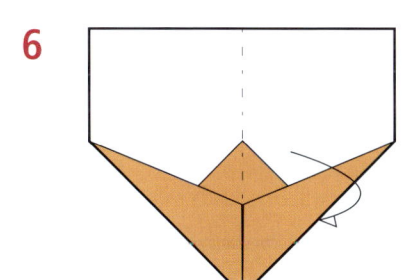

6 Fold the plane in half away from you.

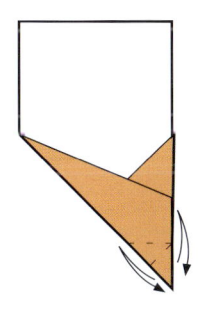

7 Fold and unfold on lines 5 and 6. Line 5 starts where the paper gets thick.

8 Put pressure on the nose of the plane to flex it open into a small scoop shape. Continue pressing to close the scoop, then pivot the resulting rhombus shape toward you so the model lies flat. Fold the tip to the right on line 7, and then fold the bottom half of the rhombus behind.

9 Fold and unfold the rudder on line 8. The tip of the rudder touches an imaginary line between the beginning of the fold and the back outside corner.

10 Reverse fold the rudder.

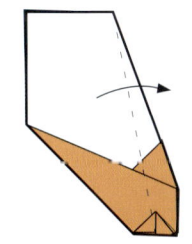

11 Fold the wings down on the 9 lines, on a line between the opening at the nose and the corner of the rudder. Straighten out the plane and you're done!

The Cadillac
BY TAKUO TODA

For a while in the 1960s, American cars were sprouting fins. The epitome was the Cadillac, with huge tail fins that were meant to make it look as sleek and powerful as a supersonic fighter jet. Now we come full circle: a jet with fins that make it look like a vintage car!

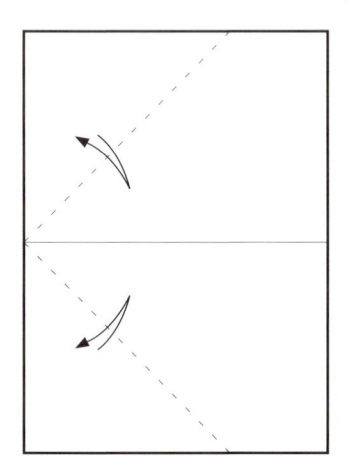

1

Start with the paper face up. Fold the left corners to the center line on the 1 lines. Unfold them again.

2

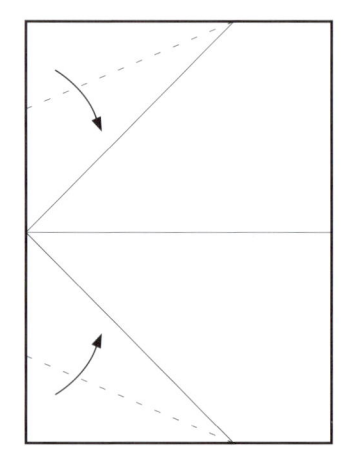

Fold the corners on the 2 lines to the creases you just made.

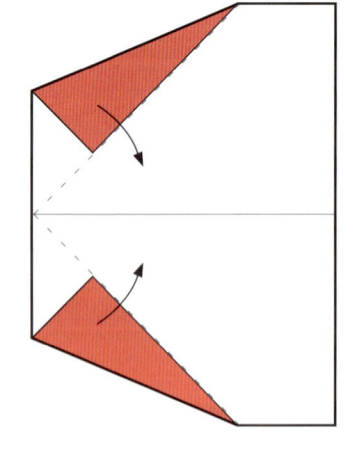

3

Refold on the 1 lines.

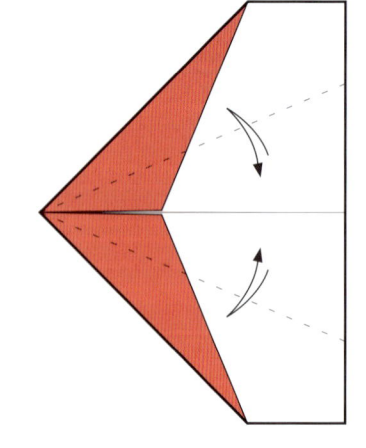

4

Fold the new corners in to the center line on the 3 lines. Unfold them again.

5

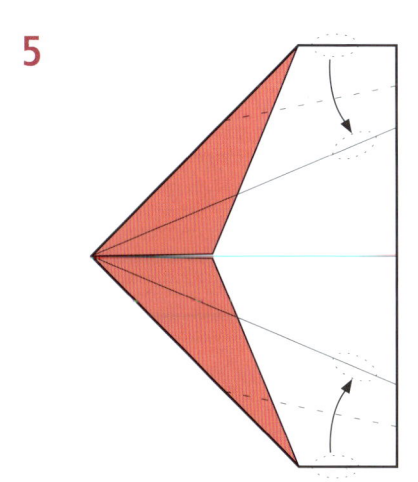

Fold the wingtips on the 4 lines so that the edges touch the new creases.

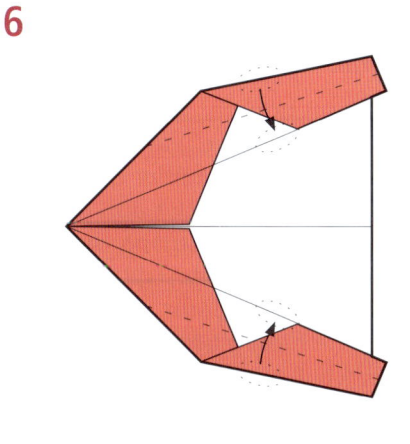

6

Fold the wingtips again the same way, on the 5 lines.

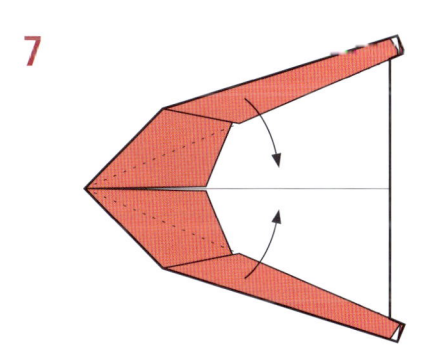

7

Refold the 3 lines.

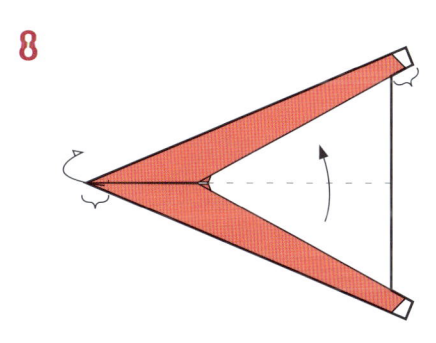

8

Mountain fold the tip of the nose at the place shown. Then fold the plane in half towards you.

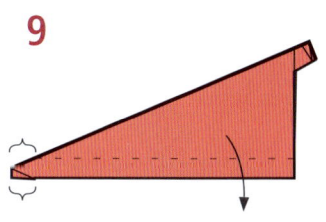

9

Fold down the wings on the 7 lines, parallel to the center line.

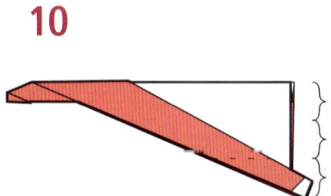

10

Fold up the wingtip rudders on the 8 lines.

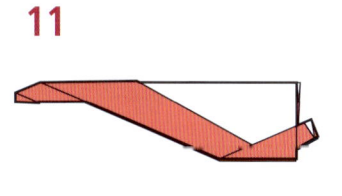

11

Straighten up the wings and rudders, and you're ready to cruise!

Icarus

BY TAKUO TODA

The Icarus is popular with kids because it is easy to fold, flies well, and looks sharp. It starts out like the familiar classroom dart, and then becomes more and more interesting. It isn't suited to strong throws, so it won't win any contests, but it is loads of fun outdoors or when flying from high places. Let the wind catch it and it'll be gone!

1

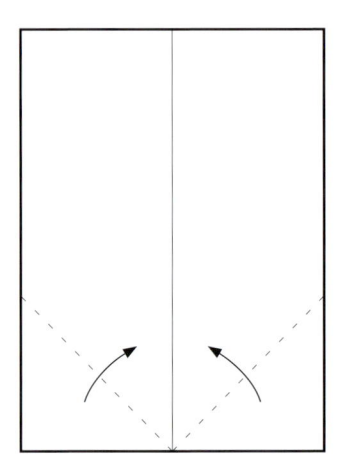

Start with the paper face down. Fold the bottom corners in to the center line on the 1 lines.

2

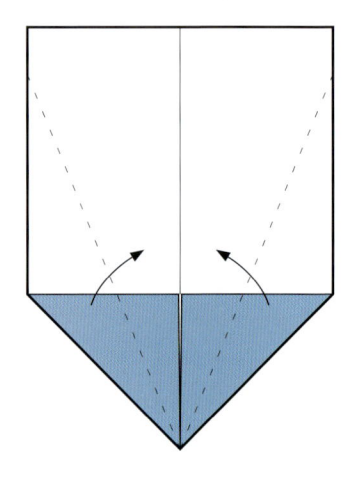

Fold the new corners in to the center line on the 2 lines.

3

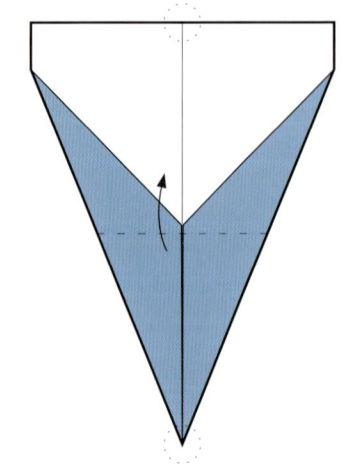

Fold the plane in half on line 3, so that the nose just touches the top edge.

4

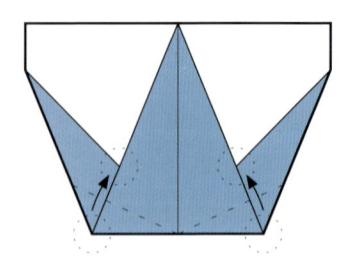

Fold the bottom corners on the 4 lines as shown. The corners should just touch the intersection of the previous two folds.

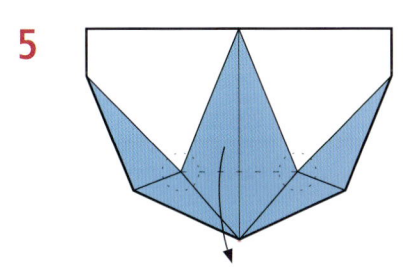

5 Fold the nose back down on line 5.

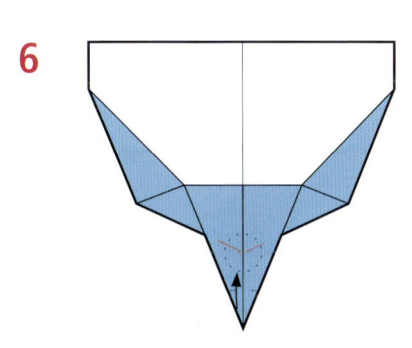

6 Fold the tip of the nose up on line 6. It should line up with the position of the edge of the paper underneath the nose.

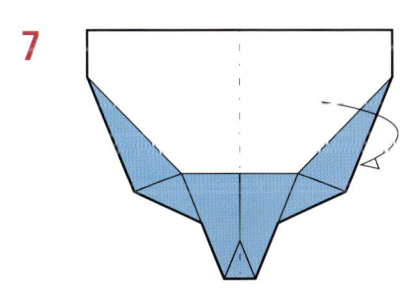

7 Fold the plane in half away from you.

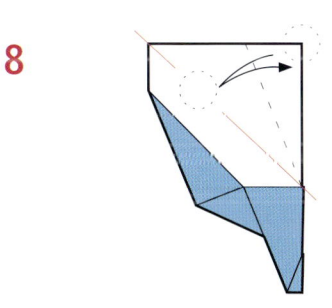

8 Fold and unfold the rudder on line 7. The tip of the rudder touches an imaginary line between the beginning of the fold and the back outside corner.

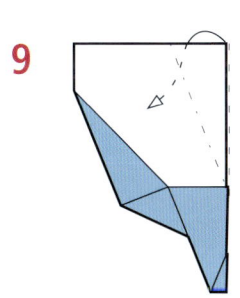

9 Reverse fold the rudder.

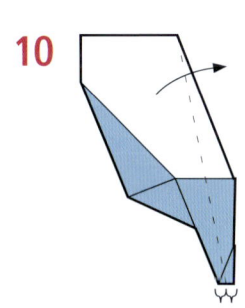

10 Fold down the wings on the 8 lines, starting at the middle of the nose and ending at the corner of the rudder.

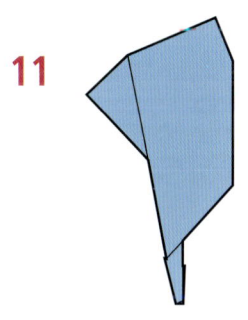

11 Straighten out the plane, bend up the back edge of the wing a little, and you're all done!

The Flying Crane
BY TAKUO TODA

The traditional origami crane can't fly, but that doesn't mean you can't fold an airplane with a crane's neck. Longer, thinner wings would have looked better, but the head and neck create a fair amount of drag, so this is the best arrangement for flying. And fly it does! It may not win prizes in a contest, but in the air it has the very same smooth and graceful glide as the real cranes swooping down from the north for the winter!

1

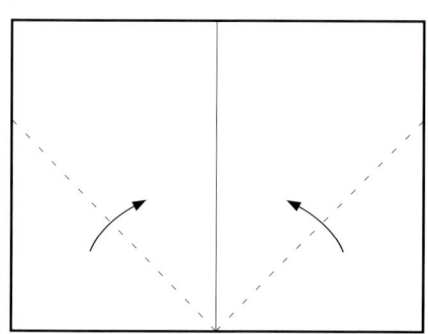

Start with the paper face down. Fold the bottom corners in to the center line on the 1 lines.

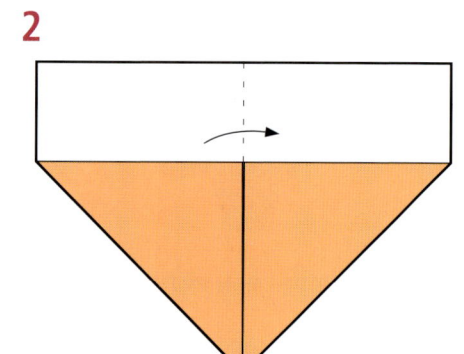

2

Fold the plane in half toward you.

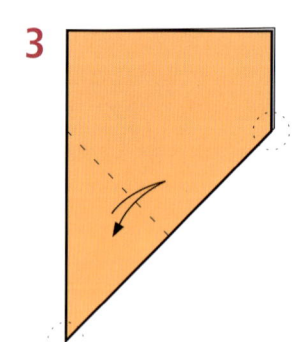

3

Fold the bottom corner up to the right hand corner on line 2. Unfold it again.

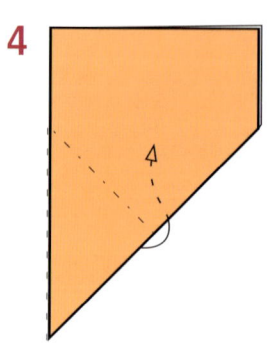

4

Reverse fold the tip inside the plane.

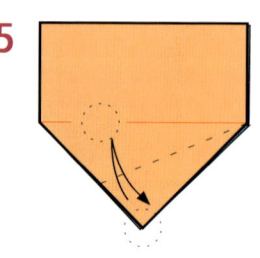

5

Fold and unfold the top flap of the bottom corner on line 3. It will touch a point on an imaginary line between the left and right hand corners. Repeat behind.

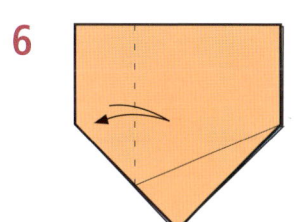

6 Fold and unfold on line 4, starting at the crease and parallel to the center line.

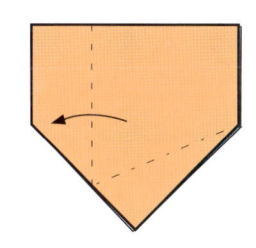

7 Open out the top layer by refolding line 4 and reversing the line 3 fold.

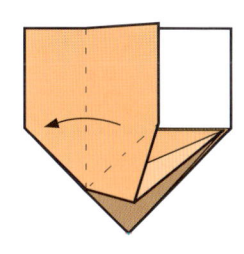

8 This is how it looks partway through the fold.

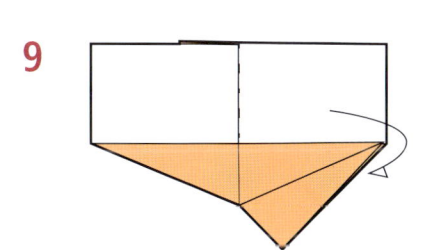

9 Repeat steps 7 and 8 for the reverse side.

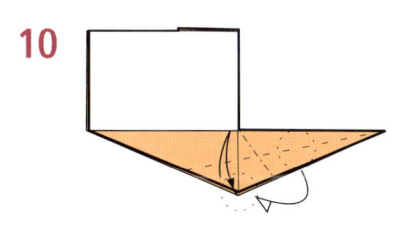

10 Fold and unfold both layers on line 5. Mountain fold the neck on line 6, so that the bottom corner touches the crease on the other side. Unfold.

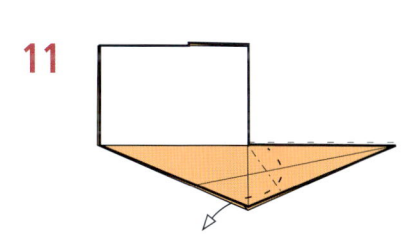

11 Reverse fold the tip on line 6.

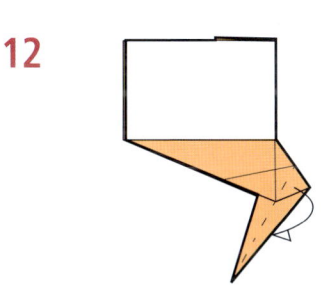

12 Tuck the loose edges inside the neck by refolding on the 5 lines.

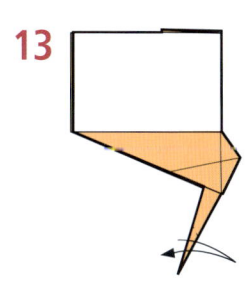

13 Fold, unfold, and reverse fold the head on line 7.

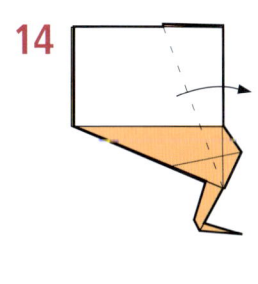

14 Fold the wings down on the 8 lines as shown.

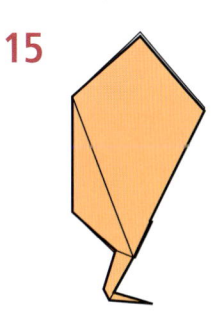

15 Straighten the plane out, bend up the rear edge of the wings sightly, and you're done.

The Zero Fighter

BY TAKUO TODA

This is the plane that set the current Guinness World Record for flight duration! The original, folded from slightly smaller A5 paper, flew 29.2 seconds indoors, which exceeded the previous record (my own Sky King) by 1.3 seconds. In order to fly that long, the plane has to be thrown as high as possible. That means it needs a lot of weight in the nose, but also the biggest wings possible. The Zero Fighter is just about ideal. How long can you make it fly?

1

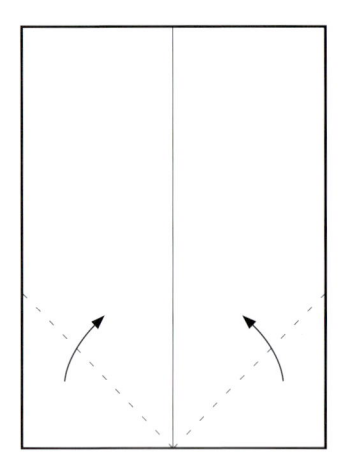

Start with the paper face down. Fold the bottom corners in to the center line on the 1 lines.

2

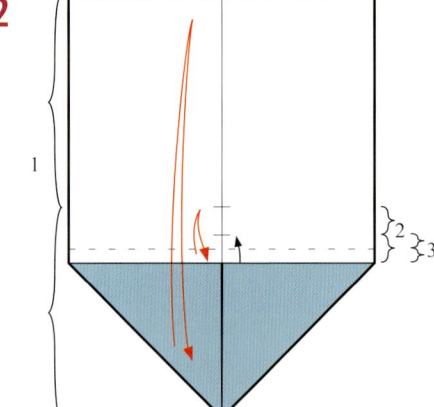

Fold the bottom half of the paper up on line 2. The fold line is one quarter of the way between the folded-up edge and the center of the paper. The red arrows show how to find the line, if using plain paper.

3

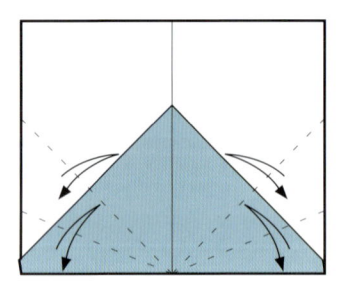

Fold the corners to the center line on the 3 lines. Unfold them, and fold the corners on the 4 lines to the creases you just made. Unfold them again.

4

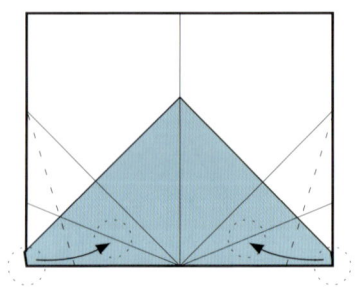

Fold the corners on the 5 lines, so that they just touch the 4 lines.

48

5

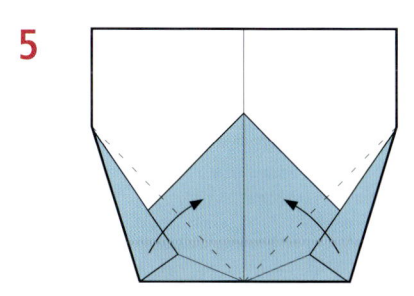

Refold the 3 lines.

6

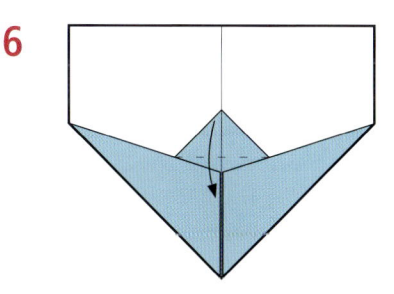

Fold the loose tip down on line 6.

7

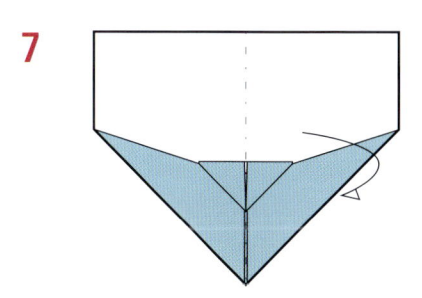

Fold the plane in half away from you

8

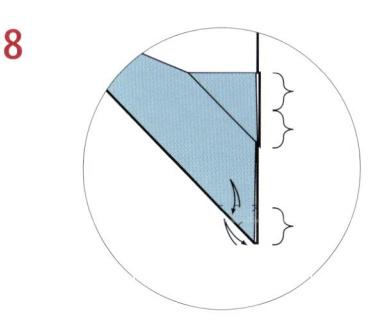

Fold and unfold the nose on lines 7 and 8. The diagram shows where line 7 begins.

9

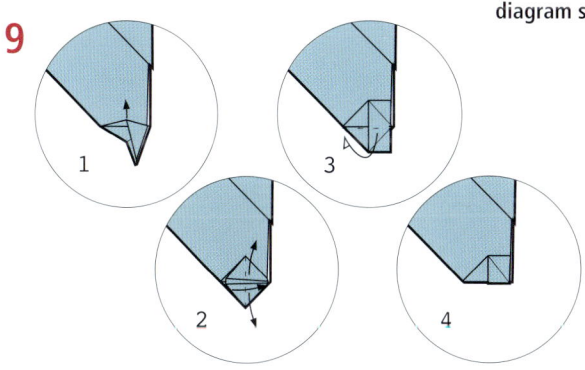

1. Put pressure on the nose so it flexes open into a small scoop shape. Press the scoop flat, then pivot the rhombus toward you so the model lies flat. 2. Lift open the pockets while you fold the free flap over to the right on line 8. 3. Fold the bottom half to the back. 4. Nose lock complete.

10

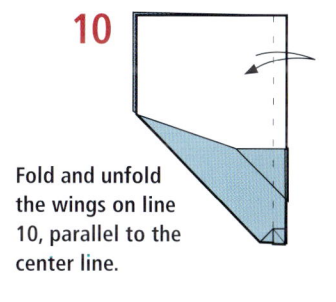

Fold and unfold the wings on line 10, parallel to the center line.

11

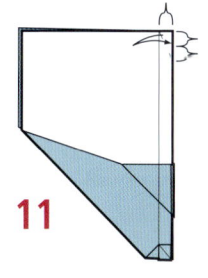

Fold and unfold the central rudder on line 11.

12

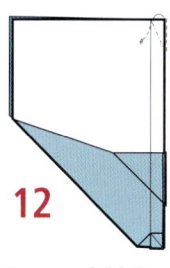

Reverse fold the central rudder.

13

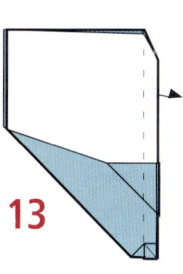

Refold the wings.

14

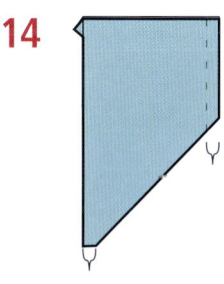

Fold up the wingtip rudders on the 12 lines. They are the same width as the fuselage. Straighten out the wings and bend up the rear edges. All done!

49

The Trident
BY TAKUO TODA

Balance and stability are always a struggle when designing paper airplanes. Planes with long noses are easy to balance, but they need very big rudders to keep from spinning and crashing, and making rudders bigger means making the back heavier again. It can become a vicious circle. But sometimes the design provides a little windfall. The Trident is like that. There's a bit of extra paper left on the top of the wings, which ends up making great fins. The three fins suggested the name, which comes from a kind of three-pronged spear.

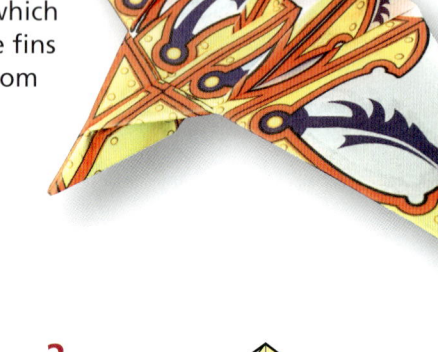

1

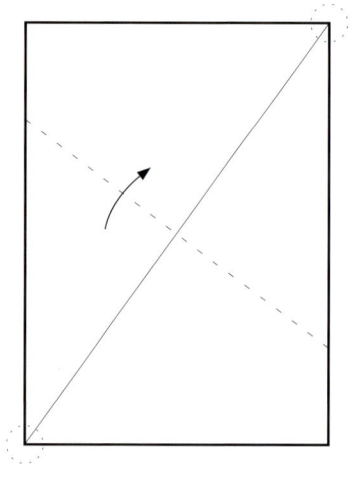

Start with the paper face down. Fold the bottom left corner to the top right corner on line 1.

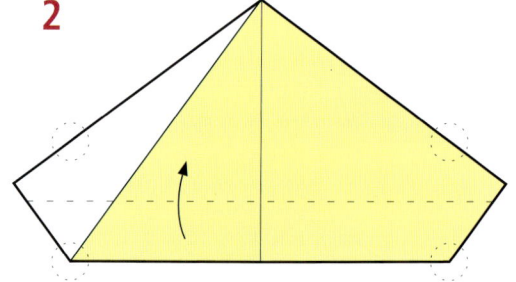

2

Turn the paper counter-clockwise slightly until it looks like this. Fold the bottom edge up on line 2 so that the corners just touch the opposite edges.

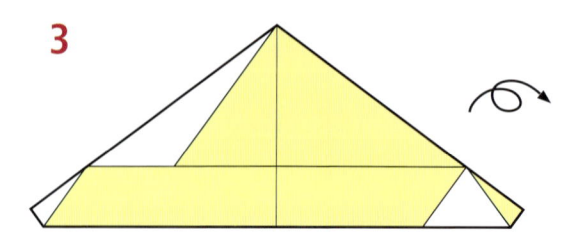

3

Here's how it will look. Flip it over.

4

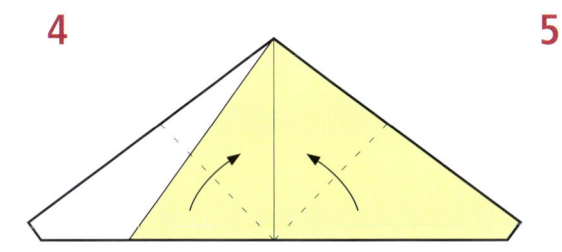

Fold the two sides up to the center line on the 3 lines.

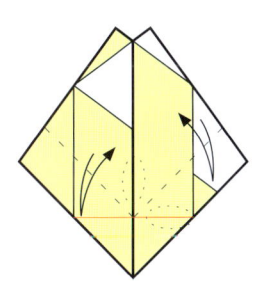

5

Fold the upper layers down on the 4 lines, starting at the center of line 5, and parallel to the sides. Unfold it again.

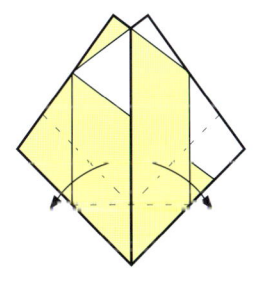

6

Refold the 4 lines as mountain folds and fold line 5. Pull the two vertical strips out and reverse fold them as you go. The next step shows how.

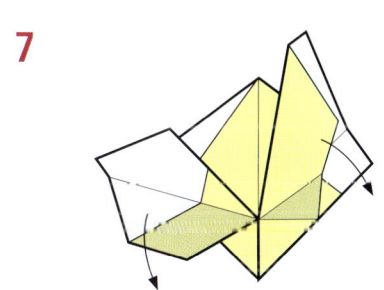

7

Here is the fold part way through: just started on the right, and almost finished on the left. These will become the wings.

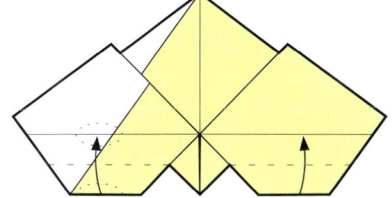

8

Once the wings are flattened out, fold the bottom edges up to the new crease on the 6 lines.

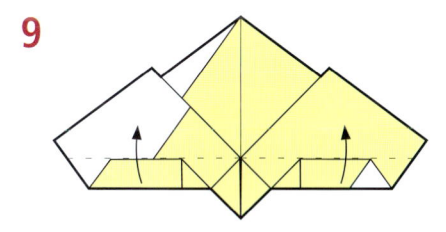

9

Refold the wing creases.

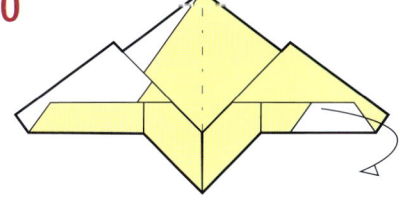

10

Fold the plane in half away from you.

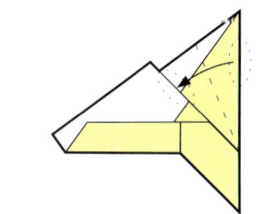

11

Fold the rudder on line 7, so the outer edge touches the edge of the wing.

51

12

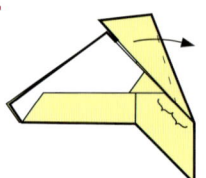

Fold the rudder back out on line 8. The diagram shows where to start the fold.

13

Unfold the rudder.

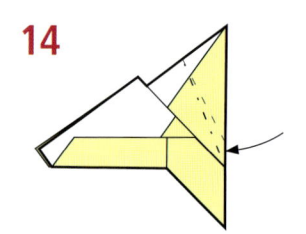

14

Double reverse fold the rudder, so that its base is inside the fuselage.

15

Pull the inside layer through to lie between the wings.

16

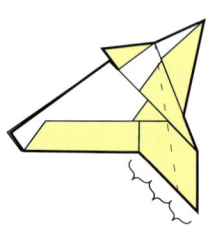

Fold the wings down on the 9 lines, starting one third of the way along the nose.

17

Fold up the small triangular flaps on each side, on the 10 lines.

18

Straighten out the plane, turn up the back edge of the wings a little, and you're done. A little tape to hold everything in place will help.

The Wave Rider

BY TAKUO TODA

Before there was a space shuttle, there were a number of experimental planes designed to explore the possibility of flying back from space. Because they would have to fly at many times the speed of sound, they had almost no wings and got their lift from the shape of their bodies. They were jokingly referred to as "potatoes with fins." But they did fly, and so does this paper version of a shockwave-riding lifting body. You'll be surprised how easy it is to fold, and how smoothly it glides across the room.

1

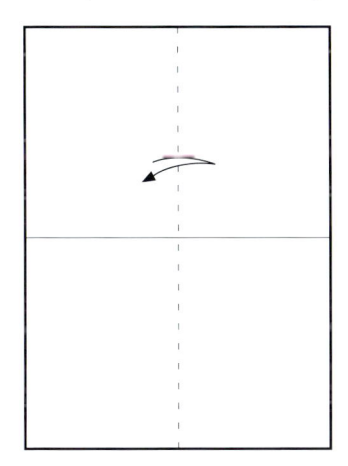

Start with the paper face down. Fold it in half on line 1, and open it out again.

2

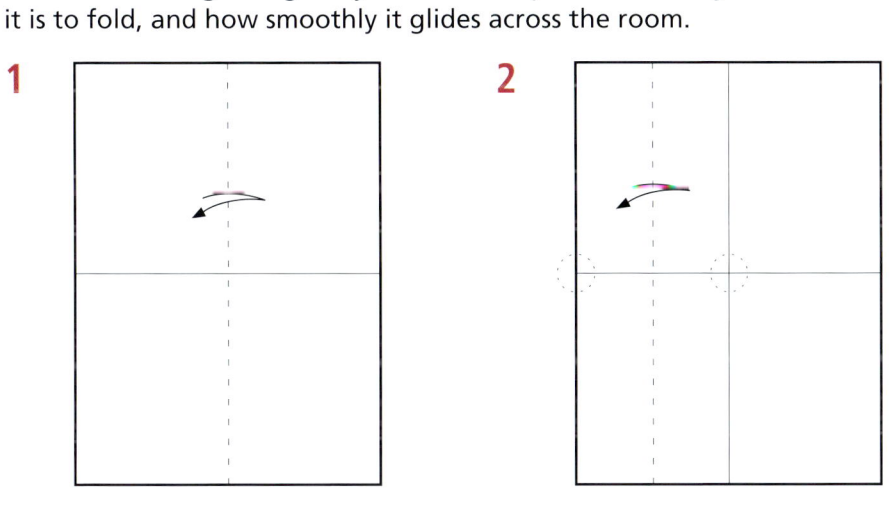

Fold the left side on line 2 to the crease you just made, and open it out again.

3

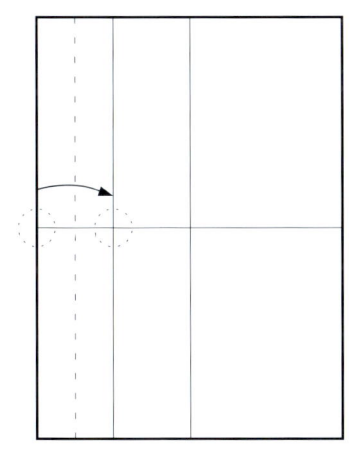

Fold the left edge on line 3 to the second crease you just made.

4

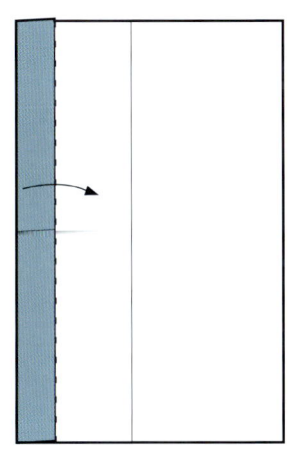

Refold on line 2.

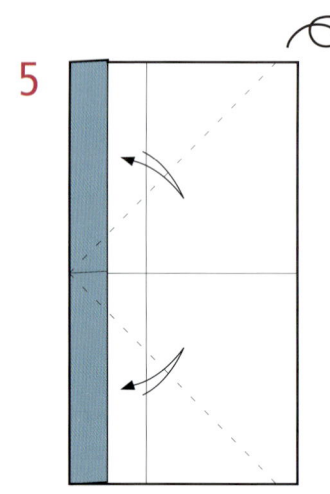

5 Fold the left hand corners in to the center line on the 4 lines, and unfold them again. Flip the paper over.

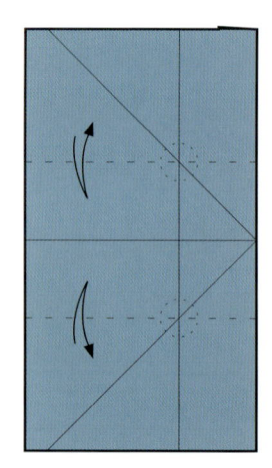

6 Fold and unfold the two sides on the 5 lines, starting at the intersection between lines 1 and 4, and parallel to the center line.

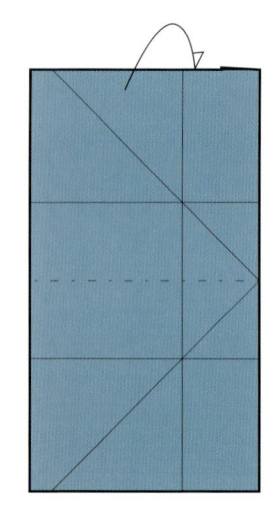

7 Fold the plane in half away from you.

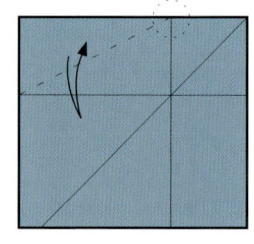

8 Fold the rudder on line 6. The diagram shows where the fold starts and ends. Unfold it again.

9 Reverse fold the rudder.

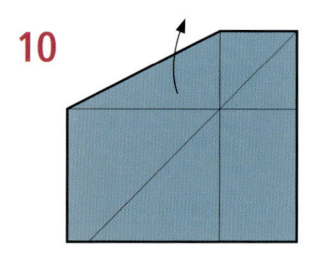

10 Unfold the plane along the center line.

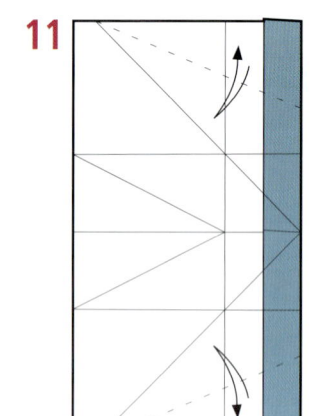

11 Fold the right corners on the 7 lines to the line 4 creases, and unfold them again.

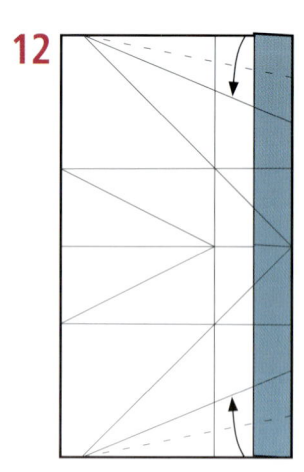

12 Fold the right corners on the 8 lines to the creases you just made.

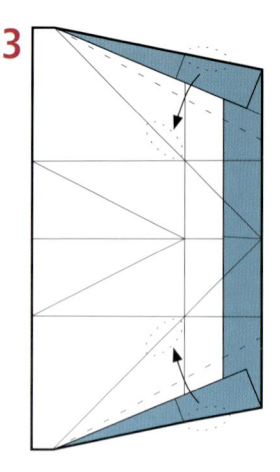

13 Fold the new edges on the 8 lines to the line 4 creases.

14

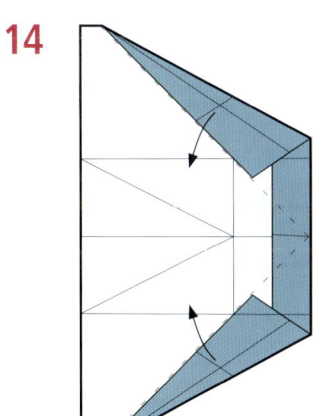

Refold the 4 lines.

15

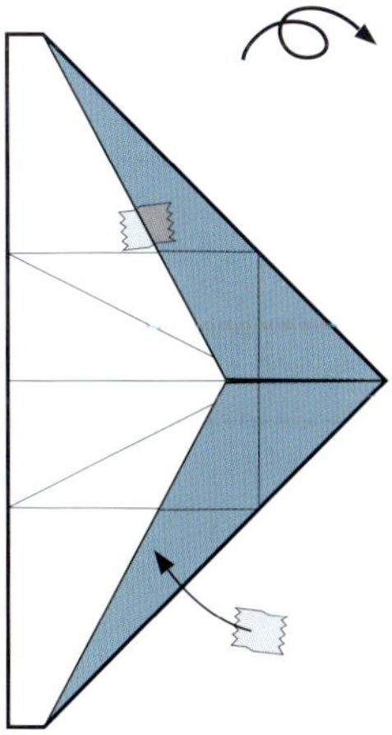

Use two small pieces of tape to hold down the folded layers. Turn the plane over.

16

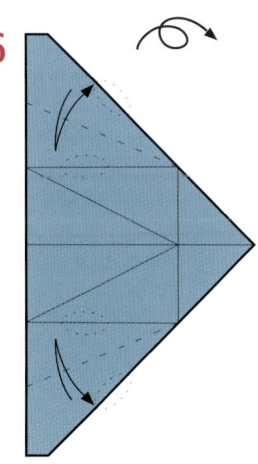

Fold the wings on the 10 lines, so that the leading edges touch the creases from the 5 folds. Unfold them again, and flip the plane over.

17

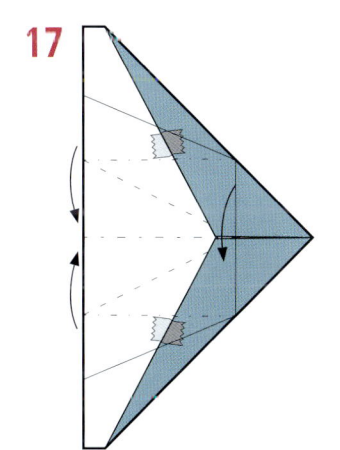

Push the two wings together so that the rudder juts out toward you and the two sides meet. One half of the nose partially overlaps the other.

18

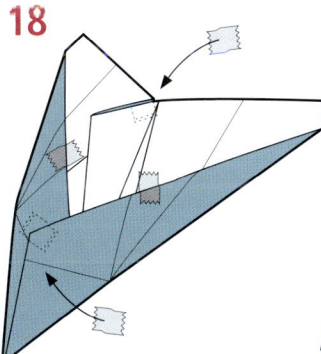

Here's what it will look like. Use a small piece of tape to hold the rudder closed. Make sure the wings aren't twisted, and tape the two nose flaps together as shown. The diagram below shows how it will look from the front.

Here is how the plane will look from the front.

19

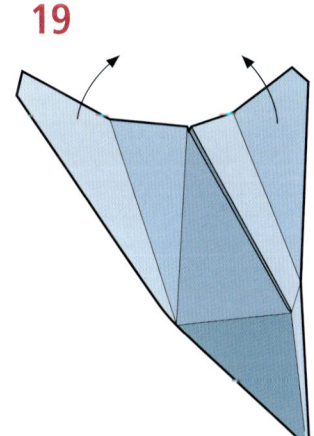

Bend the wingtips up again, and the plane is ready for launch.

55

The Ray Brick
BY TAKUO TODA

The Ray Brick is the grandfather of 3D designs. The construction of the nose is fairly straightforward, and there are no really complicated folds—just preparation for the final collapse into shape. Where does the name come from? It looks like a manta ray, and you expect it to fly like a brick. But grasp it by the stub of the rudder inside the fuselage and flick it firmly forward, and you'll see how unlike a brick it is!

1

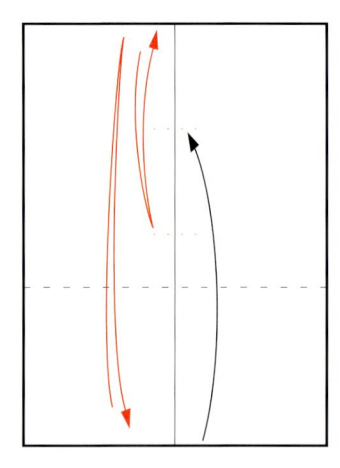

Start with the paper face down. Fold the bottom part of the paper up on line 1. The red arrows show how to find it if using plain paper.

2

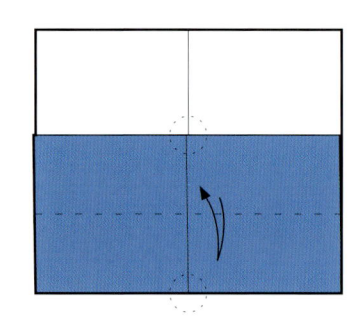

Fold and unfold the top layer on line 2.

3

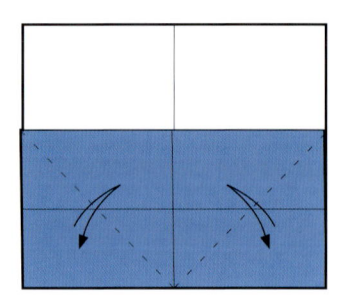

Fold the bottom corners to the center line on the 3 lines. Unfold them again.

4

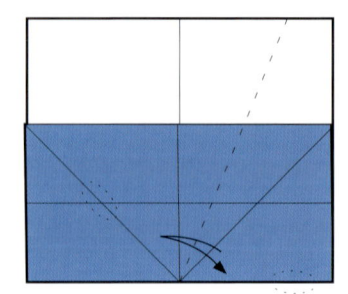

Fold the right side of the paper so that the bottom edge just touches the crease at line 3 as shown. Unfold it again.

5

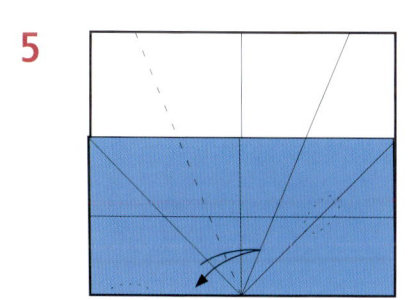

Fold the other line 4 the same way.

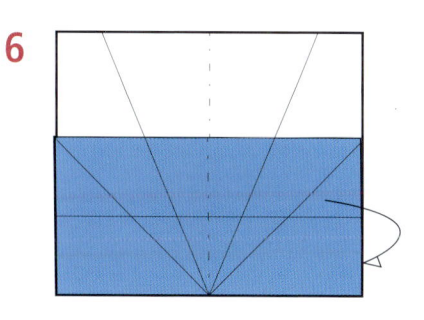

6

Fold the plane in half away from you.

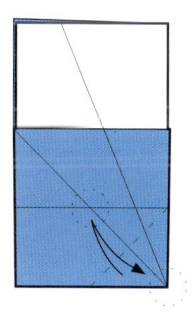

7

Fold the corner up on line 5 to the crease. Unfold.

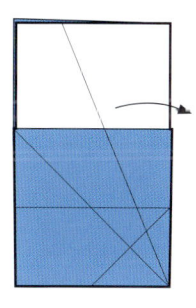

8

Open out the paper.

9

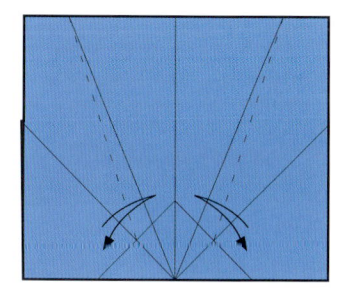

Crease the paper on the 6 lines. The diagram shows where they start and end.

10

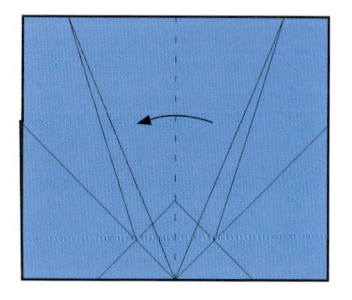

Fold the paper in half towards you.

57

11

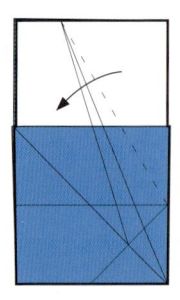

Fold the rudder on line 7 as shown.

12

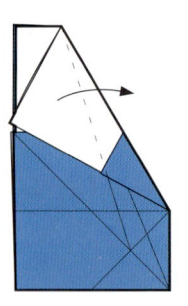

Fold the rudder back on line 8. The diagram shows where the fold starts and ends.

13

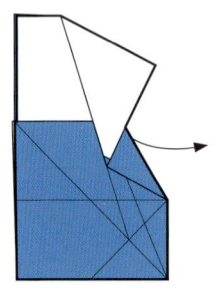

Open the paper again by pulling out the layer in back.

14

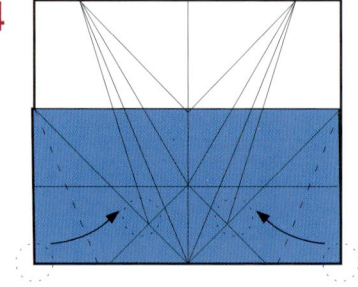

Fold the corners on the 9 lines as shown.

15

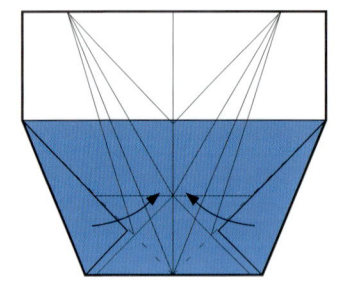

Refold the 3 lines.

16

Bend the outer panels of the wings around to the back of the plane, and put small pieces of tape over the seams to join the wings and the nose flaps.

17

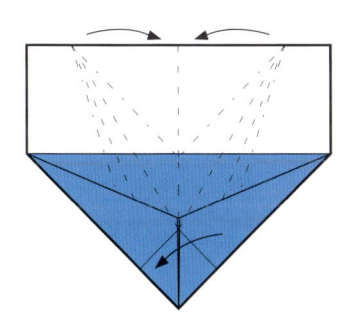

Push the two wings together so that the rudder juts out toward you and the two sides meet. One half of the nose partially overlaps the other.

18

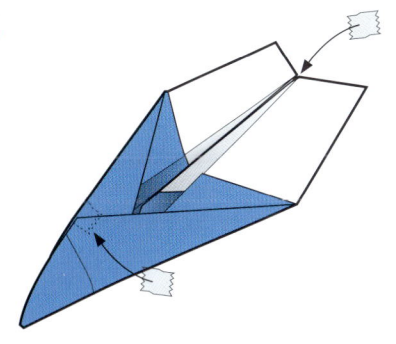

Here's what it will look like. Use a small piece of tape to hold the rudder closed. Make sure the wings aren't twisted, and tape the two nose flaps together as shown. The diagram below shows how it will look from the front.

Here is how the plane will look from the front.

59

Jupiter Space Shuttle

BY TAKUO TODA

Jupiter is based on a very old design of mine first published in 1978, even before the real space shuttle made its debut. It was the first 3D design with a cockpit. When the wingtip fins were added later for extra stability, Jupiter was born. This is the basis for the almost identical Space Glide plane that was (is!) going to be flown from the International Space Station. When that happens, it will become a celestial body in truth as well as name!

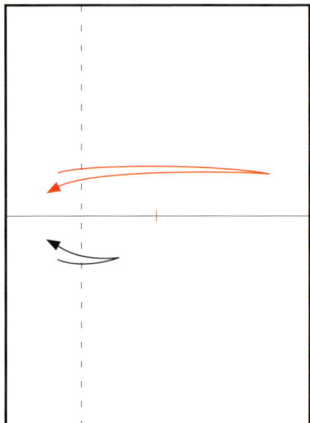

1

Start with the paper face down. Fold and unfold on line 1. The red arrows show how to find it if using plain paper.

2

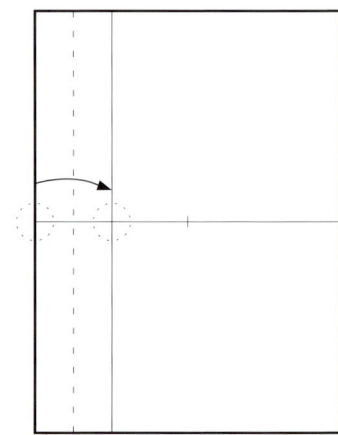

Fold the edge of the paper on line 2 to the crease you just made.

3

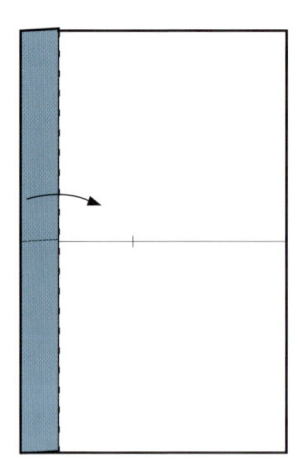

Refold on line 1.

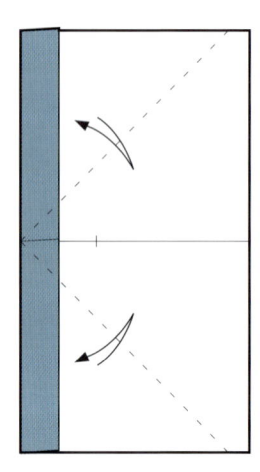

4

Fold and unfold the corners to the center line on the 3 lines.

60

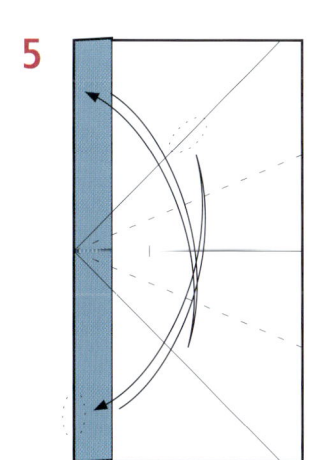

5 Fold and unfold each corner on the 4 lines, so the left edge just touches the creases you made in step 4.

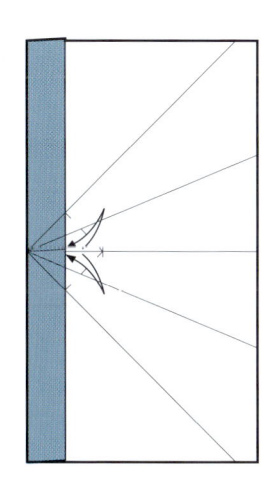

6 Crease the paper on the 5 lines. If using plain paper, they start at the mark you made in step 1 at the middle of the paper.

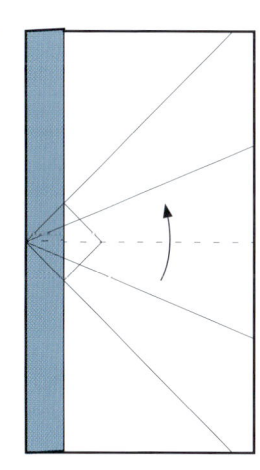

7 Fold the paper in half towards you.

8 Fold up the rudder on line 6.

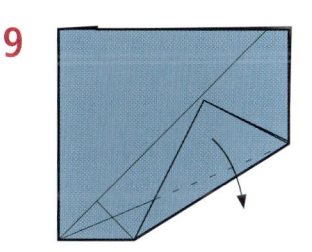

9 Fold the rudder back on line 7, matching the crease underneath it.

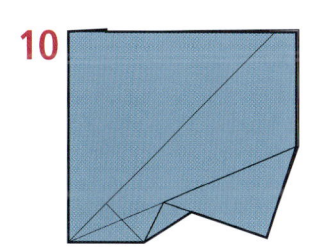

10 Double reverse fold the rudder so that it looks like diagram 11.

11 Pull out the back layer to re-open the paper.

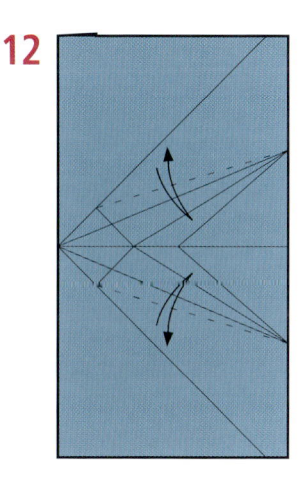

12 Crease on the 8 lines.

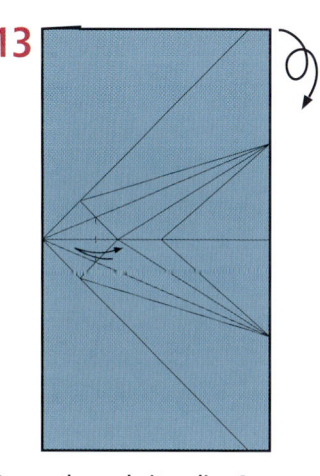

13 Crease the cockpit on line 9. Then, flip the paper top to bottom.

61

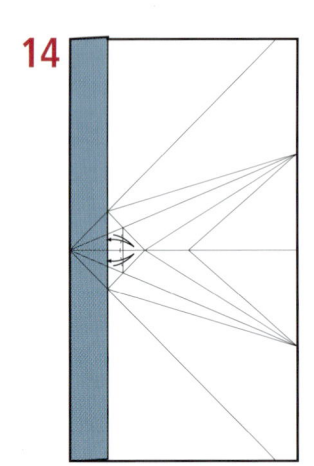

14 Crease the cockpit on the 10 lines.

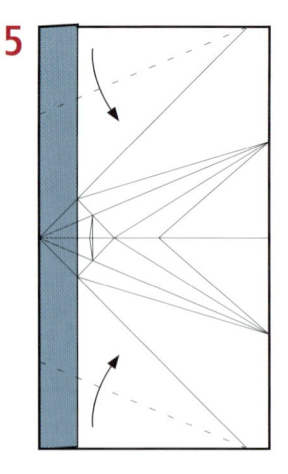

15 Fold the corners on the 11 lines, to the line 3 creases.

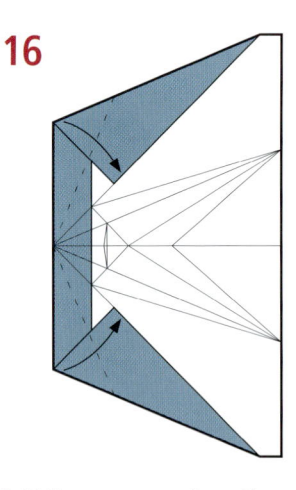

16 Fold the corners again on the 12 lines, to the 3 creases.

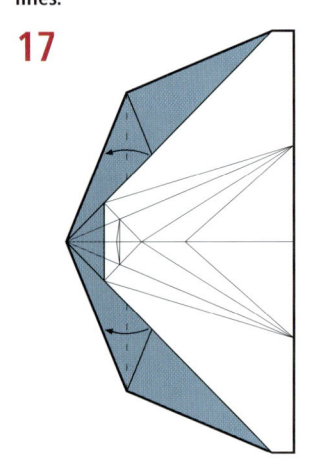

17 Fold the triangular flaps on the 13 lines.

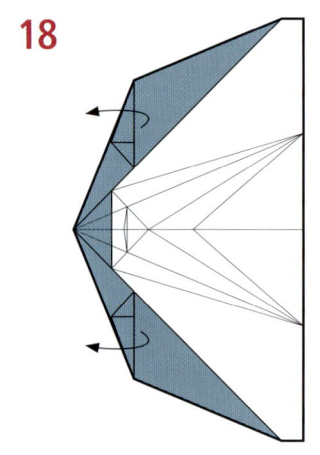

18 Pull the paper out from behind the triangles.

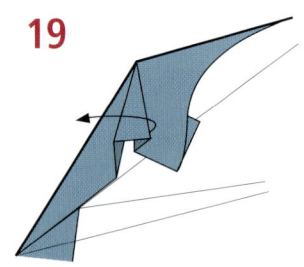

19 Refold the triangles so they stick out to the front, as shown in diagram 20.

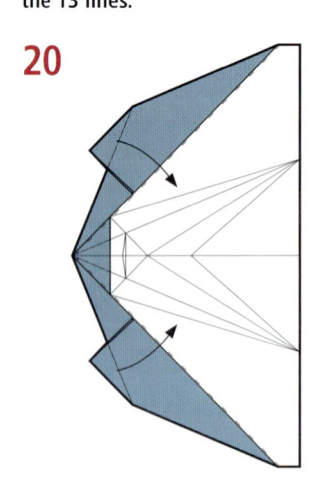

20 Refold the 3 lines.

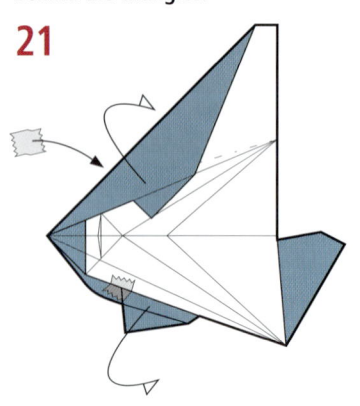

21 Bend the paper around to the back and tape the wings from the inside.

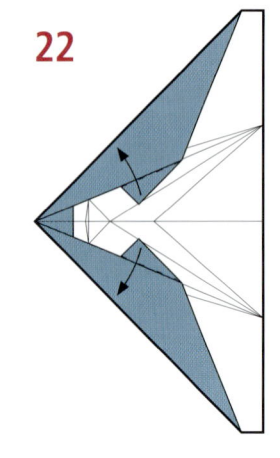

22 Fold the triangular flaps so that they stand up.

23

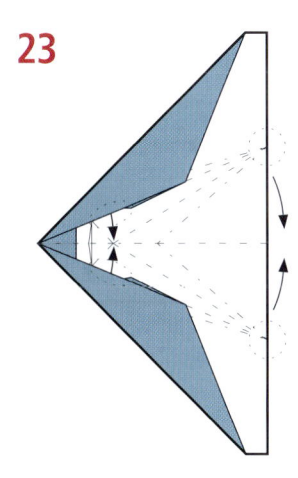

Refold the fuselage creases and push the two sides of the plane together until the triangular flaps meet.

24

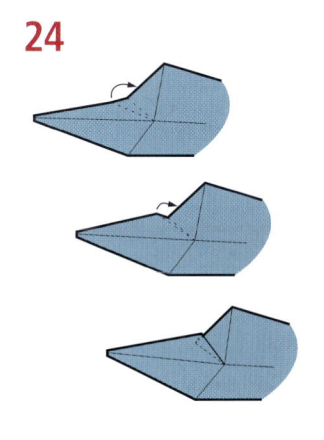

As an option, push the nose up slightly and recrease the 9 and 10 lines so that the front deck rides up over the bottom of the windshield.

25

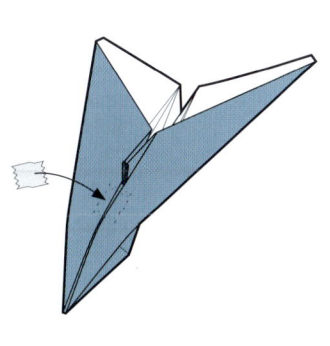

Tape the bottom of the nose together. Make sure the wings aren't twisted!

26

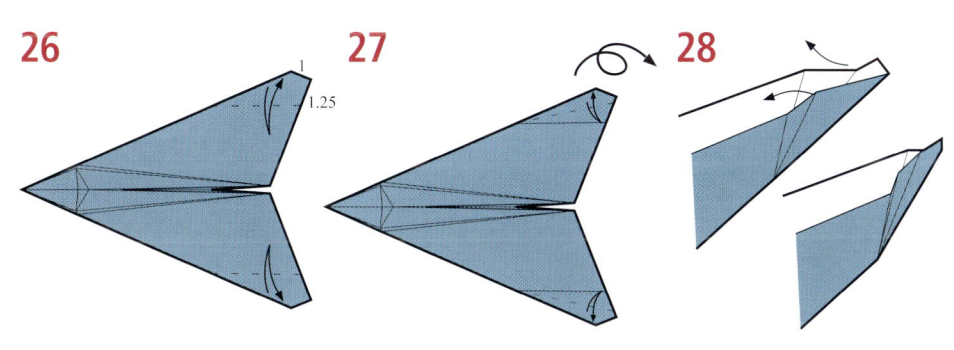

Fold and unfold the wingtips on the 14 lines.

27

Fold and unfold the wingtips on the 15 lines, so they meet the 14 line creases. Flip the plane over.

28

Squash the wingtips so that half sticks up above the wing, and half sticks down below it. Diagram 29 shows how it will look.

29

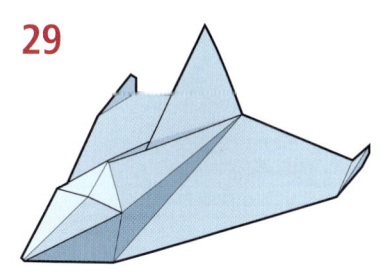

All finished!

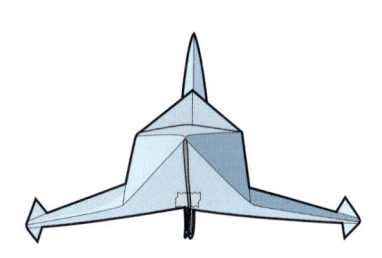

63

Published by Tuttle Publishing, an imprint of Periplus Editions (HK) Ltd.

www.tuttlepublishing.com

Copyright © 2018 Takuo Toda and Andrew Dewar

All rights reserved. No part of this publication may be reproduced or utilized in any form or by any means, electronic or mechanical, including photocopying, recording, or by any information storage and retrieval system, without prior written permission from the publisher.

Photo & Illustration Credits

Takuo Toda: 4–6, 8–11, 14–15, 17–18, 19 (top), 20–23, 31 (bottom), box bottom author photo.
Andrew Dewar: 1–3, 12–13, 16 (bottom), 25–26, 28–30, 31 (top), 32–34, 36–38, 40, 42, 44, 46, 48, 50, 52–53, 56, 59–60, box and booklet cover paper airplane photos.
All other photos as attributed. Diagrams by Andrew Dewar. Color illustrations and folding paper designs by Konstantin Vints.

ISBN 978-0-8048-4637-0

Distributed by

North America, Latin America & Europe
Tuttle Publishing
364 Innovation Drive
North Clarendon,
VT 05759-9436 U.S.A.
Tel: (802) 773-8930
Fax: (802) 773-6993
info@tuttlepublishing.com
www.tuttlepublishing.com

Japan
Tuttle Publishing
Yaekari Building,
3rd Floor, 5-4-12 Osaki
Shinagawa-ku
Tokyo 141 0032
Tel: (81) 3 5437-0171
Fax: (81) 3 5437-0755
sales@tuttle.co.jp
www.tuttle.co.jp

Asia Pacific
Berkeley Books Pte. Ltd.
61 Tai Seng Avenue
#02-12 Singapore 534167
Tel: (65) 6280-1330
Fax: (65) 6280-6290
inquiries@periplus.com.sg
www.periplus.com

First edition   22 21 20 19 18   7 6 5 4 3 2   Printed in Hong Kong   1807EP

TUTTLE PUBLISHING® is a registered trademark of Tuttle Publishing,
a division of Periplus Editions (HK) Ltd.

ABOUT TUTTLE
"Books to Span the East and West"

Our core mission at Tuttle Publishing is to create books which bring people together one page at a time. Tuttle was founded in 1832 in the small New England town of Rutland, Vermont (USA). Our fundamental values remain as strong today as they were then—to publish best-in-class books informing the English-speaking world about the countries and peoples of Asia. The world has become a smaller place today and Asia's economic, cultural and political influence has expanded, yet the need for meaningful dialogue and information about this diverse region has never been greater. Since 1948, Tuttle has been a leader in publishing books on the cultures, arts, cuisines, languages and literatures of Asia. Our authors and photographers have won numerous awards and Tuttle has published thousands of books on subjects ranging from martial arts to paper crafts. We welcome you to explore the wealth of information available on Asia at **www.tuttlepublishing.com**.